Charlotte Brontë's
Novels

ROBERT BERNARD MARTIN is Associate Professor of English at Princeton University and an expert on the Victorian era and its literature. He is the author of *The Dust of Combat: A Life of Charles Kingsley* and *Enter Rumour: Four Early Victorian Scandals.*

Charlotte Brontë's Novels

The Accents of Persuasion

ROBERT BERNARD
MARTIN

The Norton Library
W · W · NORTON & COMPANY · INC ·
NEW YORK

W. W. Norton & Company, Inc. is also the publisher of *The Norton Anthology of English Literature,* edited by M. H. Abrams, Robert M. Adams, David Daiches, E. Talbot Donaldson, George H. Ford, Samuel Holt Monk, and Hallett Smith; *The American Tradition in Literature,* edited by Sculley Bradley, Richmond Croom Beatty, and E. Hudson Long; *World Masterpieces,* edited by Maynard Mack, Kenneth Douglas, Howard E. Hugo, Bernard M. W. Knox, John C. McGalliard, P. M. Pasinetti, and René Wellek; *The Norton Reader,* edited by Arthur M. Eastman, Caesar R. Blake, Hubert M. English, Jr., Alan B. Howes, Robert T. Lenaghan, Leo F. McNamara, and James Rosier; and the NORTON CRITICAL EDITIONS, in hardcover and paperbound: authoritative texts, together with the leading critical interpretations, of major works of British, American, and Continental literature.

for
G.S.B.

'The Bells are very sincere in their worship of Truth, and they hope to apply themselves to the consideration of Art, so as to attain one day the power of speaking the language of conviction in the accents of persuasion. . . .'

[Charlotte Brontë, writing of herself and her sisters Emily and Anne, to W. S. Williams, 14 August 1848]

CONTENTS

PREFATORY NOTE

References for quotations from Miss Brontë's four novels and the three other works frequently cited are inserted directly into the text following the quotations themselves. Quotations from the novels are taken from the first editions as listed below; obvious errors in punctuation and spelling have been silently corrected. For the convenience of readers using more recent editions, modern chapter numbers are given, followed by volume and page references to first editions.

The Professor: A Tale, 2 vols. (Smith, Elder, and Co., London, 1857.)
Jane Eyre: An Autobiography, 3 vols. (Smith, Elder, and Co., London, 1847.)
Shirley: A Tale, 3 vols. (Smith, Elder, and Co., London, 1849.)
Villette, 3 vols. (Smith, Elder, and Co., London, 1853.)

Abbreviations for works frequently cited:

Gaskell   E[lizabeth] C. Gaskell: *The Life of Charlotte Brontë* (Smith, Elder, and Co., London, 1857.) Once more, modern chapter numbers precede volume and page references to the first edition.

SHB   *The Brontës: Their Lives, Friendships and Correspondence*, ed. Thomas J. Wise and J. Alexander Symington, 4 vols. (Shakespeare Head Press, Oxford, 1932.)

Shorter   Clement Shorter: *The Brontës: Life and Letters*, 2 vols. (Hodder and Stoughton, London, 1908.)

Since the book is divided into four chapters, each of which deals with one of Miss Brontë's novels, and since the same concerns with passion, imagination, moral intelligence, intellect, reason, self-knowledge, maturity, subjectivity, objectivity, etc. occur repeatedly in each chapter and form the argument itself of the book,

I have not included an index. Normally, such an omission detracts from the convenience of readers, but in this case the only index that would make complete sense would be one that included nothing but the titles of the four novels; further division, it seems to me, would only lead to obfuscation.

INTRODUCTION

With the sense of eternity upon him, King Lear referred
contemptuously to the fickleness of popularity, and those who
live by it he called 'packs and sects of great ones/That ebb
and flow by th' moon.' Such a lunar flux has scant relevance
to the esteem in which the Brontës have been held for over a
hundred years. It is now nearly a quarter of a century since
that pioneer in modern Brontë studies, Miss Ratchford,[1]
lamented the torrent of biographies of the secluded Yorkshire
family, the riddling 'Keys', 'Vindications', Freudian studies,
and the steamy plays and novels insecurely based on their
lives. So great was the number of books and monographs
that Miss Ratchford noted with an understandable weariness
that no other writers save Shakespeare and Byron had
provoked so much attention as had Charlotte and Emily
Brontë. The renaissance of interest in the Victorians
since World War II has only served to swell the rushing
stream of Brontë studies into a sometimes polemically raging
flood.

The Haworth hagiography, like other saints' legends,
serves to objectify many of the mysterious aspects of man's
life, to exemplify the influence of the dark forces swaying
that existence. Precisely because they make concrete what we
sometimes dimly suspect or fear, these writings, like other
hagiographies, have tended to be both scrupulous (even dis-
putatious) about factual detail and irresponsibly speculative

[1] Fannie Elizabeth Ratchford, *The Brontës' Web of Childhood* (Columbia
University Press, New York, 1941.)

about motive. The bare facts are so literally improbable as to tease one into considering the lives of the Brontës themselves as some wild metaphorical statement of the Romantic conception of the world. Aside from the hundreds of thousands of persons who have read *Jane Eyre* or *Wuthering Heights*, there must be an equal number of others, innocent of knowledge of the novels, who have been at least momentarily captured by the story of that gaunt parsonage and the Gothic lives of its inhabitants, and somehow made uneasy about the world in which it was played out. The fevers of Cowan Bridge; Tabby; the four children writing their stories of Angria and Gondal in the tiny room above the front door; Patrick Brontë, firing his pistols from the windows of his bedroom; the foreboding sound of the gravemason's chisel in the churchyard; Keeper's beating at the hands of Emily; Charlotte's stay in the establishment of M. Héger; the three sisters with linked arms walking endlessly around the sitting-room table; the confrontation of George Smith by Emily and Charlotte; Emily's dying gaze failing to recognize the sprig of heather brought her by Charlotte from the wintry moors; Anne's gentle fading from life at Scarborough; the fatal pregnancy that ended Charlotte's brief marriage; beyond them all the moor with its violent winds and gentle flowers, and its unchanging, recurrent cycle of seasons oblivious to the pathetic series of funeral processions as the family dwindled: the beads of the Brontë rosary slip easily through the fingers.

It would be an unimaginative mind indeed that was unstirred by the lives of the Brontës, and it would require a heart more steadfast than most would care to own to be unmoved by pity for them. Many of us have felt at some time as Swinburne did when he wrote in 1877: 'From the first hour when as a schoolboy I read *Jane Eyre* and *Wuthering Heights* I have always retained the first intense desire I felt then to know all that I might or ought to know about the two women who wrote them.' Even Matthew Arnold, whose meeting with Charlotte was a somewhat qualified success, remembered it

so vividly that it formed the centre of his elegiac poem,
'Haworth Churchyard', with its evocation of the 'sisterly
band' and

> . . . the church [that]
> Stands on the crest of the hill,
> Lonely and bleak;—at its side
> The parsonage-house and the graves.

Somewhat uncharacteristically, Arnold treated the sisters
as persons rather than as metaphors for the creative spirit,
and he was so moved by the sombre story of their lives
that his habitually reserved muse soared at the thought of
Emily,

> . . . she, who sank
> Baffled, unknown, self-consumed;
> Whose too bold dying song
> Stirr'd, like a clarion-blast, my soul.

Even the best of biography, however, may tend to serve
history rather than literature, and one may be forgiven for
wishing to return from their lives to the works of the sisters
Brontë. One of the dangers of too great absorption with the
biographies of writers is that their books are apt to be forgotten. There is another danger—and possibly a worse one—
which is that the books may become important only so far as
they can be taken as mirrors of the lives of their creators.
Either the critic stresses only those aspects of the books that
he can demonstrate as paralleling the life of the author, or he
inverts the process and searches the novels for biographical
fact, assuming that what occurs in the books must necessarily
have an exact and literal precedent in the life of the writer.
The possibility that diurnal life may undergo a sea-change in
being transformed into art is discounted.

In spite of a widely held view that none of her novels quite
equalled *Wuthering Heights*, it has been Charlotte who has
almost monopolized the biographers and critics from the

publication of Mrs. Gaskell's *Life* to the present. This state of
affairs is no doubt attributable to her life having been longer
and more public than that of her brother and sisters, and to
the fact that her correspondence has survived, as her family's
has not, so that the raw materials for biography have been
more easily available. Consequently, it has been her works
that have suffered most seriously from what might be called
the Purple Heather School of Criticism and Biography. Her
novels have been carefully documented to show the 'originals'
of characters and locales, forgetting that Miss Brontë was a
novelist, that she was neither camera nor tape-recorder, and
that her purpose was not that of documented history. It was
Charlotte Brontë herself who wrote to Ellen Nussey, warning her not to suppose that any of the characters in *Shirley*
(her only attempt at a novel with historical background) were
intended as portraits of real persons: 'It would not suit the
rules of art, nor my own feelings, to write in that style. We
only suffer reality to *suggest*, never to *dictate*. The heroines are abstractions, and the heroes also. Qualities I have
seen, loved, and admired, are here and there put in as
decorative gems, to be preserved in that setting.' [Shorter,
II:84.]

Miss Ratchford's studies of the little books that Charlotte
Brontë wrote as a child were a healthy corrective to some of
the excesses of biographical speculation, for the emphasis
was finally back on what Miss Brontë had written, rather
than on what she had been and seen. In addition, Miss Ratchford was able to show that many of the characters and situa-
tions of the novels were prefigured in the Angrian writings,
and that these antedated Miss Brontë's acquaintance with
some of the 'originals' of the novels.

Useful as these studies have been, they contain implicit
pitfalls for the critic who merely substitutes originals in the
Angrian stories for those in Charlotte Brontë's acquaintance;
in either case, little is said about the mature novels themselves. Even Miss Ratchford has sometimes fallen into the

trap for which she has provided such attractive bait. In her remarks on Dr. John Bretton[1] she identifies him as a 'Zamorna' character by his likeness to the Angrian hero-villain, and then suggests that he is a failure because he is not *totally* like Zamorna. This judgment deprives the author of the possibility of artistic (and personal) maturation, as well as negating the possibility that a character's personality and function may be considerably more complex than the germ of its inspiration. Surely, what is important here is a consideration of how adequately Dr. John fulfils his function in *Villette*, not how exactly he coincides with a character from his creator's early works.

In the past decade or so, there has been in the criticism of Charlotte Brontë, as in the criticism of other Victorian writers, an increased willingness to treat her novels as seriously conceived works of art, worthy of rigorous examination rather than rhapsodic appreciation, and deserving of a close scrutiny to determine what she has to say and the means by which she says it, how her novels manage to reduce the untidy flow of experience to the proportions and the order of art.[2]

Perhaps the conclusion to the last sentence will suggest my own attempt to answer the nagging question of what use to make of biographical material in looking at a novel. It would be a singularly foolish critic who refused to employ any tool that might be of use to him. Biography, however, may be a recalcitrant helper in understanding a work of art unless one keeps its limitations firmly in mind. It may serve to suggest why a particular character or event in a novel seemed of peculiar significance to the author, and it may point the way, therefore, to an understanding of the use she intended to make of it, but what it can never do is to show by itself the function of any part of a work of art. To put the matter in

[1] Pp. 229–34.
[2] For some of the most illuminating critical studies, see the 'Critical Bibliography'.

another way, biography may illuminate the process of creation, but it can never shed much light on the finished product.
(If this seems unkind to those fine scholars who have done so
much to document the facts of Miss Brontë's life, the slight
is unintentional, for I wish only to note the dangers of ill-
applied biography in criticism.) Experience, whether personal or vicarious, whether in 'real' life or in literature
(either the writings of other authors or the Angrian out-
pourings of one's own youth), is the material of which fiction
is made, obviously, but it need no more resemble the finished
product than a mulberry leaf is like the silk embroidery into
which it has been transformed. To point out the trees where
the leaves grew that the silkworm ate is to say little of importance about the embroidery.

It may be worth saying, however, that a comparison, or
contrast, of an event or acquaintance from the author's life
with its fictional counterpart may sometimes point the way
to an understanding of what she was attempting, and even,
occasionally, an understanding of what she did achieve. The
problem of intent, as Mr. Wimsatt has been at pains to point
out,[1] is a complicated one, and one is never justified in confusing the author's intentions with the effect of a work of art,
but an understanding of what the author was attempting to
do may often stimulate us to think about the work in ways we
might otherwise neglect.

The following study, then, is an attempt to search out the
themes that occupied Miss Brontë in her novels and to demonstrate how they are given artistic life; in short, to show how
Charlotte Brontë attempted to speak 'the language of conviction' in the 'accents of persuasion'.

*   *   *   *   *

Here I should like to record my gratitude for the helpful

[1] W. K. Wimsatt, Jr., and Monroe C. Beardsley, 'The Intentional Fallacy,' in
The Verbal Icon (University of Kentucky Press, Lexington, 1954).

kindness shown to me during the writing of this book by the
Princeton University Library, the Bodleian Library, and the
British Museum, as well as my thanks for the financial assist-
ance of the Princeton University Committee on Research.

Princeton, N.J.
March 1965

1

THE PROFESSOR

At least six publishers refused *The Professor* before Charlotte Brontë reluctantly shelved it in order to finish *Jane Eyre*, but she obviously thought well of it none the less, for she subsequently suggested that George Smith reconsider his initial refusal and publish it as a successor to *Jane Eyre*. After the publication of *Shirley* she offered her first-born to Smith a third time, but his feeling against it was still so strong that even Miss Brontë's great reputation seemed inadequate reason to accept the manuscript. Reluctantly, for she had written a preface in 1851 in the expectation of its publication, she agreed to lock *The Professor* and 'the monotony of his demure Quaker countenance' into a cupboard and forget him. But she had no intention of destroying the work, and after her death Sir James Kay-Shuttleworth and Mrs. Gaskell dug out the manuscript and together convinced Mr. Nicholls that he should consent to its publication. This time, knowing that there were to be no more novels from Currer Bell, Smith was glad to take the manuscript for his firm. The virtues that Miss Brontë found in the novel have not always been apparent to her readers, who have frequently felt it be be an undernourished, if not starved, work.

In her preface Miss Brontë wrote that her juvenile attempts before beginning *The Professor* had cured her of 'any such taste as I might once have had for ornamented and redundant composition', and that she had 'come to prefer what was plain and homely. . . .

'I said to myself that my hero should work his way through

life as I had seen real living men work theirs—that he should never get a shilling he had not earned—that no sudden turns should lift him in a moment to wealth and high station; that whatever small competency he might gain, should be won by the sweat of his brow; that, before he could find so much as an arbour to sit down in, he should master at least half the ascent of "the Hill of Difficulty"; that he should not even marry a beautiful girl or a lady of rank. As Adam's son he should share Adam's doom, and drain throughout life a mixed and moderate cup of enjoyment.

'In the sequel, however, I find that publishers in general scarcely approved of this system, but would have liked something more imaginative and poetical—something more consonant with a highly wrought fancy, with a taste for pathos, with sentiments more tender, elevated, unworldly. Indeed until an author has tried to dispose of a manuscript of this kind, he can never know what stores of romance and sensibility lie hidden in breasts he would not have suspected of casketing such treasures. Men in business are usually thought to prefer the real; on trial the idea will be often found fallacious: a passionate preference for the wild, wonderful, and thrilling—the strange, startling, and harrowing—agitates divers souls that show a calm and sober surface.' [1:v–vii]

Most readers would agree with the publishers in asking for 'something more imaginative and poetical' in the novel, although what they might mean by those notoriously slippery terms would probably be considerably different from the meaning Miss Brontë attached to them in this context. By both terms she seems to have meant that which is contrary to literal fact and probability, a meaning more often given to 'imaginative' than to 'poetical' in the popular usage of our own day.

Miss Brontë's preface makes her sound a confirmed rationalist, a term more than a little misleading when applied to the author of *Jane Eyre* and *Villette*. It is a cliché to say that her first and third books tried for the look of a transcription of everyday life, while the second and fourth used the trappings of the Gothic and proceeded from a sensibility that attempted to unite the claims of both the rational and non-rational faculties of man. For the truth is that Charlotte Brontë never finally decided on the relative values of the claims of these two parts of man's mind; in her best works it is the tension that exists between their opposing pulls that gives the novels their vitality, and the resolution of the problem that gives the reader a sense of fulfilment.

In her preface to *The Professor* she was clearly thinking of the imagination and the poetic faculties as non-rational processes and therefore without any real validity; on occasion, when particularly worried about the harmful effects of relying on the imagination, she equated it with undisciplined wallowing in emotion and sentiment, and consequently thought it something to be feared and avoided. The very fear of what she thought of as the imagination is some measure of the attraction she felt for it, and a recognition of its necessity for her. *The Professor* is, in part, a repudiation of its preface, for Miss Brontë was unable to avoid showing the necessity of the emotions. In *Jane Eyre* and *Villette* she transcends this distrust of the non-rational and, with a more mature attitude to the imagination, makes the theme of both novels the reconciliation of the head and the heart into the kind of superior cognition or imagination that Coleridge meant when he wrote of the 'secondary Imagination', which 'dissolves, diffuses, dissipates, in order to recreate; . . . it struggles to idealize and to unify'.[1] What Coleridge meant was the essentially creative power that gives embodiment to the perceptions of man's mind, that power that makes an artistic unity out of the disparate, discrete aspects of life, and at her greatest, this is what Miss Brontë was able to do with the

[1] *Biographia Literaria*, ed. J. Shawcross, 2 vols. (Clarendon Press, Oxford, 1907), 1: 202.

extraordinary hodge-podge of emotions and experiences that
are the raw material of her novels.

Since she failed to keep *The Professor* as unemotional a tale
as she planned, it is not surprising that Miss Brontë's preface
seems disingenuous or, at least, indicative of less than the
whole truth of her attitudes. Nor was it only within the
framework of her novels that she felt the necessity for something beyond a literal, factual view of the world. The 'imaginative and poetical' aspects of the Angrian tales and of her
other juvenilia are well-known. When she was only eighteen,
she prepared a reading list for her friend Ellen Nussey. The
list itself is not exceptional, for the poets she recommends
include the names one would expect a well-read young
lady of the early part of the century to know, including
Shakespeare, of course, with Milton, Wordsworth, and most
of the major poets between them. Significantly, however, the
only times her enthusiasm is roused are when she is writing
of Shakespeare and Byron ('Both these were great men, and
their works are like themselves') and of 'Scott's sweet, wild,
romantic poetry.' 'For fiction,' she wrote, 'read Scott alone;
all novels after his are worthless.' [Gaskell, Chap. 7, I:140.]

Perhaps even more revealing than her early love of these
three writers, with all the romantic feeling implied thereby,
are her mature views on Jane Austen, a writer whose themes,
if not style, one might expect her to admire. In January 1848
she wrote to G. H. Lewes, who had said that he would rather
have written *Pride and Prejudice* or *Tom Jones* than any of
Scott's Waverley novels: 'I had not seen "Pride and Prejudice" till I read that sentence of yours, and then I got the
book. And what did I find? An accurate, daguerreotyped
portrait of a commonplace face; a carefully-fenced, highly-
cultivated garden, with neat borders and delicate flowers;
but no glance of a bright, vivid physiognomy, no open
country, no fresh air, no blue hill, no bonny beck. I should
hardly like to live with her ladies and gentlemen, in their
elegant but confined houses.' [Gaskell, Chap. 16, II:54.]

A week later she indignantly answered Lewes, quoting his own dictum: ' "Miss Austen is not a poetess, has no 'sentiment' (you scornfully enclose the word in inverted commas), no eloquence, none of the ravishing enthusiasm of poetry," and then you add, I *must* "learn to acknowledge her as *one of the greatest artists, of the greatest painters of human character*, and one of the writers with the nicest sense of means to an end that ever lived." ' [Gaskell, Chap. 16, II:55.] It is the very lack of poetry and sentiment that keeps Jane Austen from the greatness of George Sand and Thackeray, she told Lewes: 'Miss Austen being, as you say, without "sentiment", without *poetry*, maybe *is* sensible, real (more *real* than *true*), but she cannot be great.' [Gaskell, Chap. 16, II:56.]

Miss Brontë's misunderstanding of her great predecessor is less interesting for its indication of her failure as a critic than it is for its implications of the type of sensibility she felt in her own writing. Two years later she tried reading Jane Austen once more, but she had to admit to W. S. Williams that she still felt greatly dissatisfied:

'I have likewise read one of Miss Austen's works—*Emma*—read it with interest and with just the degree of admiration which Miss Austen herself would have thought sensible and suitable. Anything like warmth or enthusiasm—anything energetic, poignant, heart-felt is utterly out of place in commending these works: all such demonstration the authoress would have met with a well-bred sneer, would have calmly scorned as outré and extravagant. She does her business of delineating the surface of the lives of genteel English people curiously well. There is a Chinese fidelity, a miniature delicacy in the painting. She ruffles her reader by nothing vehement, disturbs him by nothing profound. The passions are perfectly unknown to her; she rejects even a speaking acquaintance with that stormy sisterhood. Even to the feelings she vouchsafes no more than an occasional graceful but distant recognition—too frequent converse with them would ruffle the smooth elegance of her progress. Her business is not half so much with the human heart as with the human eyes, mouth, hands, and feet. What sees keenly, speaks aptly, moves flexibly, it suits her to study; but what throbs fast and full, though hidden, what the blood rushes through, what is the unseen seat of life and the sentient target of death—this Miss Austen ignores. She no more, with her mind's eye, beholds the heart of her race than each man, with bodily vision, sees the heart in his heaving breast. Jane Austen was a complete and most sensible lady, but a very incomplete and rather insensible (*not senseless*) woman. If this is heresy, I cannot help it. If I said it to some people (Lewes for instance) they would directly accuse me of advocating exaggerated heroics, but I am not afraid of your falling into any such vulgar error.' [Shorter, II:127-8.]

It seems, then, in spite of her preface that Miss Brontë was violating her own most deeply held convictions when in writing *The Professor* she 'restrained imagination, eschewed romance, repressed excitement,' avoided 'over-bright colouring', and 'sought to produce something which should be soft, grave, and true'. [Gaskell, Chap. 16, II:42.] What is most important about this transgression against her own instincts is that it indicates a good part of the reason the novel lacks the artistic unity of the later works. When Miss Brontë eschewed imagination in her sense of the word, with its connotations of excess, exaggeration, and improbability, she failed to fulfil the claims of the Imagination, as Coleridge used the term. The true unity of a work of art eluded her at the very time she sought to find it by emphasis on a single aspect of perception. Paradoxically, it was when she was most eclectic in her choice of material that her work was most unified in effect, and the more literally improbable those materials the greater the sense of reality she achieved. As Lord David Cecil has written, 'Out of her improbabilities and absurdities, she constructed an original vision of life; from the scattered, distorted fragments of experience which managed to penetrate her huge self-absorption, she created a world.'[1]

The world of Charlotte Brontë's novels is, to be sure, a circumscribed one when compared to the worlds of Shakespeare or Chaucer or Milton or even that of her admired master, Thackeray, but the breadth of the world the artist dreams has little relationship to our sense of fulfilment in it. Completeness is all. The horizons may be narrow, but one must have a sense of the artist's having explored them. In spite of *Shirley*, one does not go to Charlotte Brontë for an understanding of Victorian history or politics; the wise man repairs to her novels for an exploration of her own confined world, and it is only when one feels that she has attempted to close a curtain over half that world, as in *The Professor*, that one feels its cramping limits.

The plot of *The Professor* is a simple one, organized in linear, chronological fashion with three settings, the central section in Brussels sandwiched between two English sections. Crimsworth quarrels with the brother who employs him, goes to Brussels as a schoolmaster, is attracted by Mlle. Reuter, falls in love with Frances, marries her and eventually takes her back to England. Once Crimsworth has seen through the wiles of Mlle. Reuter, he embarks upon his courtship of Frances, which is carried through without hitch or complication. It is improbable that the story has often held children from play or old men from the chimney corner.

It has been customary to say of the novel, taking the lead from Miss Brontë's husband's postscript to her preface, that it is a kind of preliminary sketch for *Villette*. True, the two novels are set in Brussels, there is a professor-student relationship that develops into love, and the inhabitants of the Pension Héger have been reworked into fictional being in both novels; but these are mere surface resemblances, and in reality the first novel has less likeness to *Villette* than has

---

[1] *Early Victorian Novelists: Essays in Revaluation* (Constable and Co., London, 1934), p. 125.

Jane Eyre. What is most interesting about it as a first novel is the introduction of themes that characterize the rest of the novels. All too often, however, the techniques were not yet developed for giving life to these themes.

Since Miss Brontë spent so much of her life in either preparation for or the practice of teaching, it is hardly surprising that all four of her novels are concerned with pedagogues and pupils, with master-disciple relationships, with learning to know oneself and the world. It may reasonably be objected that most novels share in a concern so generally stated as this last, but Miss Brontë's novels are, strictly speaking, novels of development, in which the learning process develops an inexperienced or unfinished character into a mature person. In *The Professor* and *Villette*, the central pair of characters are both teachers; in *Jane Eyre* the eponymous character is teacher, then governess; in *Shirley* Louis Moore is a tutor. However, the relationship between master and pupil is not always a neat parallel for the learning process of life. Jane Eyre, for instance, is technically the teacher, but in the initial stages of their relationship, it is Rochester who educates her. Then the roles are reversed, and he becomes the pupil as she becomes the dominant member of the pair. Lucy Snowe is both school-mistress and pupil, but M. Paul learns from her as much as he is able to teach her.

At its core *The Professor* has a triangle of teaching and learning. Hunsden acts as worldly monitor to Crimsworth, who in turn educates Frances in English and in life and love. But it is Frances who acts as arbiter and teacher to Hunsden in the ways of the heart.

Hunsden's method of instructing Crimsworth is rough, almost insulting in the fashion that characterizes the relationship of men in Miss Brontë's novels. (After this first attempt she wisely followed the example of Jane Austen in avoiding scenes in which only men appear.) In the early scenes in X——, Hunsden is set in marked contrast to Edward Crimsworth; where Hunsden is brusque in his machinations to aid

William Crimsworth, Edward Crimsworth is brutal in his treatment of his brother. Like two contrasting parts of his personality, Hunsden and Edward struggle to dominate William Crimsworth. At the beginning of the book William is put in the position of having to choose to be like either his aristocratic mother or his plebeian father. His brother has settled for vulgar tradesman's ideals combined with the haughtiness of the would-be aristocrat: the worst of two worlds. Hunsden has the ascetic habits and the Olympian contempt of vulgarity that accords with his ancient lineage, but he combines them with an innate modesty that prompts him to profess being only a tradesman and a hater of the upper classes. As passion dominates Edward Crimsworth, so a slightly vinegarish, somewhat spinsterish, dispassionate rationality animates Hunsden. Edward hates his brother because he recognizes in him an innate aristocracy that he lacks himself, Hunsden berates William Crimsworth for the same sort of oversensitivity that he perceives in the aristocratic face of the portrait of his mother. Edward Crimsworth tries to crush the humanity in his brother, Hunsden liberates that humanity by freeing it of pretension.

In the later part of the book Edward Crimsworth's passionate anger and arrogance is replaced as a menace to William by the sexual licence of Pelet, who tries to make the Englishman his disciple. In this part of the book the ascetic Hunsden is set in contrast to Pelet. Like most of the sensualists in Miss Brontë's novels, Pelet is guileful, shifty, untrustworthy. Mlle. Zoraïde is the feminine equivalent of Pelet, and their marriage is the matching of like characters. Miss Brontë was not so unsubtle as to suggest that either passion or reason existed without dilution in persons, but she so feared the deleterious effect of passion that she believed it could negate reason or even pervert it into craftiness. Crimsworth says of Zoraïde: ' "To read of female character as depicted in Poetry, and Fiction, one would think it was made up of sentiment, either for good or bad—here is a specimen, and a most sensible and respectable specimen, too, whose staple ingredient is abstract reason. No Talleyrand was ever more passionless than Zoraïde Reuter!" So I thought then; I found afterwards that blunt susceptibilities are very consistent with strong propensities.' [Chap. 10, I:175–6.]

However necessary reason may be to curb passion, the man deficient in the proper passion was a poor man to Charlotte Brontë. Nor did she attempt to put a Victorian disguise on the fact that a controlled sexual passion is the normal manifestation of the well-adjusted personality. Hunsden, in spite of the coolness with which he can diagnose Crimsworth's failures in self-analysis, fails himself to understand half of life. Overt sensuality he can comprehend intellectually, but the sexuality that shares a happy tenancy of man's body, mind, and emotions with the intellect, he cannot understand. His influence over Crimsworth lessens as the tutor falls in love with Frances. Crimsworth knows that his friend cannot understand his animal nature or his love for the young teacher: 'Keen-sighted as he was, [he could not] penetrate into my heart, search my brain, and read my peculiar sympathies and antipathies; he had not known me long enough, or well enough, to perceive how low my feelings would ebb under some influences, powerful over most minds; how high, how fast they would flow under other influences, that perhaps acted with the more intense force on me, because they acted on me alone. Neither could he suspect for an instant the history of my communications with Mdlle. Reuter; secret to him and to all others was the tale of her strange infatuation: her blandishments, her wiles . . . had changed me, for they had proved that I *could* impress. A sweeter secret nestled deeper in my heart; one full of tenderness and as full of strength. . . .' [Chap. 22, II:129.]

Like St. John Rivers in *Jane Eyre*, Hunsden is left at the end of the novel with nothing but the portrait of the woman he loves, dependent upon other relationships for affection, cut off from the proper fulfilment of his life. As an example to

Crimsworth, he has stood for the necessity of reason and for the insufficiency of that faculty as a complete guide to life.

Crimsworth's relationship with Frances is deliberately opposed to those with his pupils and with Mlle. Reuter. As his best pupil, Frances is contrasted to the other students, whose superior she is in both intellectual and emotional capacity. The coarseness and vulgarity of the majority of the pupils are exemplified in the occupants of the first bench, Eulalie, Hortense, and Caroline, and in the other three fledgling sensualists, Aurelia, Adèle, and Juanna. To their mean spirits are contrasted the Protestant intelligence, good manners, and modesty of Frances. The opposite extreme in his pupils is the embryo nun, Sylvie, 'gentle in manners, intelligent in mind'. Nationality and religion bring out the innate sensuality of the others, but in Sylvie they have stifled the normal growth: 'her physical organization was defective; weak health stunted her growth and chilled her spirits. . . . She permitted herself no original opinion, no preference of companion or employment; in everything she was guided by another. With a pale, passive, automaton air, she went about all day long doing what she was bid; never what she liked, or what, from innate conviction, she thought it right to do. The poor little future religieuse had been early taught to make the dictates of her own reason and conscience quite subordinate to the will of her spiritual director. She was the model pupil of Mdlle. Reuter's establishment; pale, blighted image, where life lingered feebly, but whence the soul had been conjured by Romish wizard-craft!' [Chap. 12, 1:202–3.]

Sylvie and Frances are drawn as the only pupils capable of intellectual achievement, but the compositions of Sylvie are coldly and unimaginatively correct whereas those of Frances are lit by an inquiring spirit and warmed by emotion, since she unites reason and a healthy passion. 'I knew how quietly and how deeply the well bubbled in her heart,' writes Crimsworth; 'I knew how the more dangerous flame burned safely under the eye of reason; I had seen when the fire shot up a moment high and vivid, when the accelerated heat troubled life's current in its channels; I had seen reason reduce the rebel, and humble its blaze to embers. I had confidence in Frances Evans; I had respect for her, and as I drew her arm through mine, and led her out of the cemetery, I felt I had another sentiment, as strong as confidence, as firm as respect, more fervid than either—that of love.' [Chap. 19, II:50–51.] Unlike Sylvie, who remains wan and pinched, Frances gradually develops physically as she comes under the influence of Crimsworth, her figure ripens into a 'plumpness almost embonpoint [sic]', her eyes quicken, and he notices 'the exquisite turning of waist, wrist, hand, foot and ankle'. [Chap. 18, II:5.] When Crimsworth first realizes that he is falling in love with her, he notes coolly that she is 'for a sensualist charmless', [Chap. 19, II:50] but when he confesses that love for the first time, he remarks the change that love has made in both of them: 'I derived a pleasure, purely material, from contemplating the clearness of her brown eyes, the fairness of her fine skin, the purity of her well-set teeth, the proportion of her delicate form; and that pleasure I could ill have dispensed with. It appeared, then, that I too was a sensualist, in my temperate and fastidious way.' [Chap. 23, II:174.]

It has frequently been noted that one of the peculiarities of the structure of the novel is that Frances Henri does not make her unobtrusive and nameless entry into the story until almost half-way through the book, but what is usually overlooked is that her entrance is strategically placed. Released from the surveillance of Hunsden in Brussels, Crimsworth has begun to fall under the spell of the enigmatic Mlle. Reuter, and the early part of his stay in the city is primarily concerned with his learning the potence of her physical attraction. With a frankness unusual in the period, Miss Brontë shows the strongly sexual nature of a wholly decent young man. That he has gone too far in his dreams of possessing Zoraïde is made clear by his overhearing the conversation in the garden as she and her lover, Pelet, take a midnight stroll. He recovers from his infatuation that night, and the next morning he meets Frances for the first time. The rest of the novel is taken up with the development of love between a couple who, in Miss Brontë's favourite word, 'suit' each other.

The superficial likenesses between Frances and Zoraïde are almost as obvious as their basic differences, even to the point of Frances' growing to resemble the older woman in her 'embonpoint'. Ultimately, both marry pedagogues and both successfully run their own schools; the natures of the two women are, however, totally different. Initially, in her infatuation with Crimsworth, Mlle. Reuter is imperious, clearly set upon being the dominant member of the pair. When she recognizes his disdain, she becomes even more infatuated, but she changes from mistress to slave, a metamorphosis that almost converts Crimsworth into a tyrant: 'I had ever hated a tyrant; and, behold, the possession of a slave, self-given, went near to transform me into what I abhorred! There was at once a sort of low gratification in receiving this luscious incense from an attractive and still young worshipper; and an irritating sense of degradation in the very experience of the pleasure. When she stole about me with the soft step of a slave, I felt at once barbarous and sensual as a pasha.' [Chap. 20, II:83.]

To Miss Brontë love and marriage had meaning only when they were the union of equals in independence. Unlike Zoraïde, Frances becomes more, not less, independent as she falls in love. Far from being a sultan's favourite (a description that Jane Eyre later is to apply contemptuously to her position if she were to live unmarried with Rochester), Frances brings to her marriage to Crimsworth fortune and worldly accomplishments comparable to his own, for, like Jane and perhaps Lucy Snowe, she can marry only when she is an independent woman. The subservience of woman Miss Brontë rejected, but not always her intellectual inferiority.

The novels indicate a highly traditional view of the relative intellectual abilities of man and woman, for man is clearly intended to guide the destinies of his mate, so long as he is morally equipped to do so. Because Zoraïde dominates Pelet, their marriage will probably be, within three months' time, 'a practical modern French novel'. [Chap. 20, II:90.]

Since Frances is not passion's slave, she can afford to meet Crimsworth in circumstances that must have seemed daring to Victorian readers. With no apparent sense of transgressing the normal social code, Frances entertains Crimsworth alone in her apartments. Actually, it is not easy to be sure whether Miss Brontë was completely ignorant of contemporary conventions (which seems unlikely), or whether she deliberately intended these interviews to contrast with the interviews of Crimsworth and Zoraïde, which degenerate into flirtation and, one supposes, would turn into seductions if Crimsworth were not so firmly virtuous and Zoraïde not so intent on capitalizing on all her advantages.

Frances, who has been in some ways the unconscious teacher of her own master, speaks out boldly in arguing with Hunsden after she has attained emotional and intellectual maturity. When he tells her that there is no logic in her, she retorts: 'Better to be without logic than without feeling. . . . I suppose you are always interfering with your own feelings, and those of other people, and dogmatizing about the irrationality of this, that, and the other sentiment, and then ordering it to be suppressed because you imagine it to be inconsistent with logic.' [Chap. 24, II:198–9.] Earlier in the novel Zoraïde's dominance of passion warps her intellect; at the conclusion Hunsden demonstrates that his neglect of the softer side of man's nature may lead to a perversion of the emotions. His treatment of the Crimsworths' son, Victor, tends in effect to foster the sparks of his 'temper–a kind of electrical ardour and power . . . Hunsden calls it his spirit, and says it should not be curbed.' [Chap. 25, II:254.] As we leave the novel, the last words belong to Victor, who is about to undergo the same process that his father has passed through, that of learning self-discipline and a nice adjustment of reason and passion, the education, as Miss Brontë saw it, of the sons and daughters of Adam.

The obvious crudities of *The Professor* are many, both stylistic and structural. For example, the book is riddled with the insecurity of syntax that always bedevilled Miss Brontë, and with her misguided insertions of schoolgirl French. Occasionally, she is so misled by her enthusiasm for her second language that she translates expressions she has already given in English, as when she writes of the closing of 'the school-year (l'année scolaire).' [Chap. 20, ii:74.] Since she never completely mastered colloquial conversation, it is not surprising that in this first book there are many speeches as stilted as Crimsworth's description of Frances as 'my little wild strawberry, Hunsden, whose sweetness made me careless of your hot-house grapes.' [Chap. 24, ii:183.]

The linear movement of the plot saves Miss Brontë from gross errors of construction, although one can hardly avoid irritation at such awkward devices as the letter that opens the book, outlining the necessary background material to a correspondent known only as 'Charles', who is never again mentioned. There are other maladroit touches in Miss Brontë's descriptions when she appears unable to decide whether to speak in the voice of Crimsworth recounting a simple history or with the detached, reflective tones of the novelist consciously considering the craft of fiction while exploiting a position of uninvolvement with the action. There have been notable novels (most often with novelists as protagonists) in which the problem of turning experience into fiction becomes part of the novel itself, but they have a considerably more complex viewpoint than Miss Brontë is attempting in this novel. Rather, she occasionally slides awkwardly from first person narrator into the part of omniscient narrator, with no consequent gain in effect. When Crimsworth first becomes aware of Frances, he describes her at length; then, without warning, the voice of the tutor is confused with that of the novelist: 'Now, reader, though I have spent a page and a half in describing Mdlle. Henri, I know well enough that I have left on your mind's eye no distinct picture of her; I have not painted her complexion, nor her eyes, nor her hair, nor even drawn the outline of her shape. You cannot tell whether her nose was aquiline or retroussé, whether her chin was long or short, her face square or oval; nor could I the first day, and it is not my intention to communicate to you at once a knowledge I myself gained by little and little.' [Chap. 14, 1:245–6.] In *Jane Eyre* and *Villette* Miss Brontë is more subtle in her exposition, and is content to let the reader share the discoveries of her narrator without calling attention to the fact that direct information is being given.

When Crimsworth goes to Belgium, it is the occasion for a setpiece of description introduced without any attempt at disguise. 'Reader, perhaps you were never in Belgium? Haply you don't know the physiognomy of the country? You have not its lineaments defined upon your memory as I have them on mine?' Crimsworth tells us that four pictures line the wall of his memory: the first three are Eton, X———, and Belgium: 'As to the fourth, a curtain covers it, which I may hereafter withdraw, or may not, as suits my convenience and capacity. At any rate, for the present it must hang undisturbed.' [Chap. 7, 1:102–3.] Presumably convenience and capacity were lacking, for of the fourth picture we are never told, although one assumes it to be the Crimsworth house in England at the end of the book. The author's red herrings succeed only in calling unproductive attention to herself and in distracting the reader from his involvement in the novel.

In both these excerpts Miss Brontë addresses 'Reader', with a consequent lowering of emotional temperature. In *Jane Eyre* she learned to use this form of direct address cunningly, by keeping it within the framework of the narrator's personality, making it part of the spontaneous feminine outburst of a woman so overcome by the remembered emotion of her girlhood that she cannot help speaking simply and directly, with total disregard for the conventions of fiction. The effect in *Jane Eyre* is precisely the reverse of that in *The Professor*, for it serves to involve the reader in shared experience. By reserving direct address for emotional climaxes, she is able to achieve such immediacy as that of her most famous line, 'Reader, I married him.' In her first book she has not yet mastered the technique.

The choice of Crimsworth as narrator is a serious handicap to the book, for Miss Brontë was unable to impart a believable virility to her masculine mouthpiece, while the point of view of the novel denies her the opportunity of entering the mind of the chief feminine character to carry out the detailed investigation of the feminine psyche at which she was to excel. It is true that Rochester, the brothers Moore, and even M. Paul are in part quite as unbelievable as Crimsworth, but they do not fail as characters, since they are men as seen through a woman's eyes; in the three last novels it is the credibility of the feminine central consciousness (even in *Shirley*, ostensibly told in the third person) that matters, not that of the men it perceives. When the credibility of the central consciousness is open to question, as it is with Crimsworth, the reader is unable to accept the validity of his perceptions. At the same time it is clear that Miss Brontë does not intend the awareness of the narrator to be different from that of herself or of the reader.

*   *   *   *   *

Were it to serve a point, the list of flaws in the novel might be greatly extended, for it is so full of minor faults that it is doubtful that it would attract many modern readers if it were not the first published work of a great writer. Perhaps even greater flaws, however, are some of the very aspects that make the novel fascinating to lovers of the later books: the subjects that so absorbed Charlotte Brontë that she was unable to leave them out, in spite of not yet knowing how to integrate them into the plot and the themes of the novel. Awkward, intrusive, they are unassimilated diversions that impede the course of the central narrative but show clearly and naïvely the preoccupations that she was subsequently to handle with assurance.

The extended description in Chapter 23 of the hypochondria that overcomes Crimsworth is an example of the intrusive concern that is introduced into the novel without any apparent relevance. In the later books Miss Brontë introduces hypochondria, too, but she is careful to make it a symbolic physical manifestation of the ill-health of the psyche too dominated by passion; here Crimsworth's psychic health has never been better, and the reader is left puzzled.

The importance of the sexual relationship in *The Professor* scarcely needs underlining; what has already been said about the courtship and marriage of Crimsworth and Frances is sufficient indication of Miss Brontë's concern with it. The major theme of all the novels is the study of the adjustment between the reason and the passions, and the plot embodying that theme is always a love story, resulting in the marriage of the main characters in three of the novels; in *Villette* there is no wedding, but the stage is set for it, the characters prepared, the conflicts resolved, and all that remains is for the fates to be propitious. It is this insistence on a love match (but one far removed from those in the novels of her contemporaries) that makes the works of Miss Brontë seem so feminine that today it is difficult to see how any of her original readers could have thought Currer Bell a man. For her love was indeed woman's whole existence.

Miss Brontë's intimate correspondence is full of the dread of being a spinster, both because of the personal incompleteness it entailed and because of the scorn in which spinsters were held by their society. The old maids in *Shirley* are evidence of her lively compassion for such women, figures of fun, laughed at for wanting a husband, ridiculed for failing to find him. It would be unjust to suggest that her personal concern made her exaggerate the plight of spinsters, for they crowd the fiction of the period, either comic like Dickens's Miss Wardle or pathetic like Mrs. Gaskell's Miss Mattie. Even Crimsworth, sympathetic as he is in general (since he normally voices Miss Brontë's own opinions), reflects society's attitude in part: 'Look at the rigid and formal race of old maids—the race whom all despise; they have fed themselves, from youth upwards, on maxims of resignation and endurance. Many of them get ossified with the dry diet; self-control is so continually their thought, so perpetually their object, that at last it absorbs the softer and more agreeable qualities of their nature; and they die mere models of austerity, fashioned out of a little parchment and much bone. Anatomists will tell you that there is a heart in the withered old maid's carcass—the same as in that of any cherished wife or proud mother in the land. Can this be so? I really don't know; but feel inclined to doubt it.' [Chap. 23, II:154.)

Because marriage meant so much to her, Miss Brontë's standards for it were almost impossibly high. Few of the marriages in her novels are happy ones save those of the central characters. Perhaps it is not irrelevant to her feeling that marriage is not an automatically happy institution, to note that she turned down at least three proposals herself before accepting Mr. Nicholls. Passion there must be in marriage, but it was no more self-sufficient there than in any other relationship. Rochester pays cruelly for thinking that it is enough, and Crimsworth, in contemplating marriage, thinks to himself: 'I know that a pretty doll, a fair fool, might do well enough for the honeymoon; but when passion cooled, how dreadful to find a lump of wax and wood laid in my bosom, a half idiot clasped in my arms, and to remember that I had made of this my equal—nay, my idol—to know that I must pass the rest of my dreary life with a creature incapable of understanding what I said, of appreciating what I thought, or of sympathising with what I felt!' [Chap. 12, 1:215.]

As Crimsworth's equal and idol, Frances is still submissive to him as master of her mind and heart. Miss Brontë was occasionally impatient with Milton's view of the order of the sexes, but in her heart she was in agreement with him, for all her heroines look to their lovers for domination in one form or another. Probably the best statement of her attitude is not her own but her mother's, in one of the delightful love-letters she wrote to Patrick Brontë before their marriage: 'It is pleasant to be subject to those we love, especially when they never exert their authority but for the good of the subject.' [Shorter, 1:38.] Charlotte Brontë herself wrote that 'It is natural to me to submit, and very unnatural to command.' [Gaskell, Chap. 11, 1:255–6.] When she finally decided to accept Nicholls, somewhat to the dismay of her friends, the real reason for her acceptance was that suggested by Mrs. Gaskell, who told John Forster that Miss Brontë could never have been happy were she not 'well ruled and ordered' by an 'exacting, rigid, law-giving, passionate' husband. [SHB, IV:118.]

Miss Brontë's counter for virility in the novels is usually the rather brutal brusqueness of the men to the women they love. Crimsworth is as harsh to Frances at moments as Rochester is to Jane, M. Paul to Lucy, and the Moore brothers to Shirley and Caroline. When Crimsworth praises the work of his pupil, he deliberately does so in 'dry and stinted phrase', [Chap. 18, II:2] but in the autobiographical poem that Frances writes, she indicates that she sees beyond his manner:

> He yet begrudged and stinted praise,
> But I had learnt to read
> The secret meaning of his face,
> And that was my best meed.
>   [Chap. 23, II:159]

Just as the heroines of the novels learn that superficial good looks are not necessary in the men they love, so they must learn that softness is not necessarily the best indication of love. Crimsworth says of his own brusqueness: 'I like un-exaggerated intercourse; it is not my way to overpower with amorous epithets, any more than to worry with selfishly im-portunate caresses,' [Chap. 23, ii:168] and even in his initial declaration of love, he interrupts the perplexed Frances, whenever she lapses into her native French, with the com-mand, 'English!' Obviously, the half-playful reproof is meant affectionately, but even after marriage he insists on his own language: 'Talk French to me she would, and many a punish-ment she has had for her wilfulness. I fear the choice of chas-tisement must have been injudicious, for instead of correcting the fault, it seemed to encourage its renewal.' [Chap. 25, ii:225.] To the last he is as much pedagogue as lover.

Cruelty is, of course, far different from the virile brusque-ness of Miss Brontë's male characters. 'I was amused,' she wrote of a friend, 'by what she says respecting her wish that, when she marries, her husband will, at least, have a will of his own, even should he be a tyrant. Tell her, when she forms that aspiration again, she must make it conditional: if her husband has a strong will, he must also have strong sense, a kind heart, and a thoroughly correct notion of justice; be-cause a man with a *weak brain* and a *strong will*, is merely an intractable brute; you can have no hold of him; you can never lead him right. A *tyrant* under any circumstances is a curse.' [Gaskell, Chap 16, ii:21–22.]

Man's heavy-handed treatment of his woman in the novels is frequently reminiscent of the rough love-making of Shakespeare's Hotspur, and the spirit of the ladies sometimes reminds one, too, of the pertness with which Lady Hotspur responds to her husband in the assurance of his love. In ex-plaining why she was unable to accept the proposal of Henry Nussey, Miss Brontë outlined her views of the way a woman should be able to behave in a happy marriage: 'I had a kindly leaning towards him, because he is an amiable and well-disposed man. Yet I had not, and could not have, that intense attachment which would make me willing to die for him; and if ever I marry, it must be in that light of adoration that I will regard my husband. Ten to one I shall never have the chance again; but *n'importe*. Moreover, I was aware that he knew so little of me he could hardly be conscious to whom he was writing. Why! it would startle him to see me in my natural home character; he would think I was a wild, romantic enthusiast indeed. I could not sit all day long making a grave face before my husband. I would laugh, and satirize, and say whatever came into my head first. And if he were a clever man, and loved me, the whole world, weighed in the balance against his smallest wish, should be light as air.' [Gaskell, Chap. 8, 1:186.]

In the other novels the hard-edged jesting serves as a two-sided exploration by the lovers in passing through acquaintance and friendship to love; Jane Eyre's pertness, for example, is indication that she is not wounded by Rochester's abruptness. In *The Professor* the reader frequently winces at the brusqueries of Crimsworth because Frances remains such a passive character. Although the reader knows that Crimsworth does not intend to wound Frances, her behaviour is not sufficient indication that she has not been hurt, and her consciousness remains closed to the reader because of the first-person narration of Crimsworth.

The curious passivity with which Frances accepts the brusqueries and finally the love of Crimsworth is far less interesting than the gusts of headlong adoration, displays of temper, and prudent second thoughts through which the feminine characters in the other novels pass on their way to love and marriage, but it is at least an accurate representation of one aspect of Miss Brontë's attitude towards love, the 'rational' aspect. In discounting the 'imaginative and poetical' in the novel she endowed her heroine with the caution that she advised Ellen Nussey to acquire before marriage, advising her not to wait for 'une grande passion', which is only another name for 'une grande folie':

'Did you not once say to me in all childlike simplicity, "I thought, Charlotte, no young lady should fall in love till the offer was actually made?" I forget what answer I made at the time, but I now reply, after due consideration, Right as a glove, the maxim is just, and I hope you will always attend to it. I will even extend and confirm it: No young lady should fall in love till the offer has been made, accepted, the marriage ceremony performed, and the first half-year of wedded life has passed away. A woman may then begin to love, but with great precaution, very coolly, very moderately, very rationally. If she ever loves so much that a harsh word or a cold look cuts her to the heart she is a fool. If she ever loves so much that her husband's will is her law, and that she has got into a habit of watching his looks in order that she may anticipate his wishes, she will soon be a neglected fool.' [Shorter, I:197.] Fortunately for us all, Miss Brontë did not extend her own cautious viewpoint to her heroines in the three later novels.

An almost Puritan contempt for physical beauty, whether feminine or masculine, permeates the novels. Only in *Shirley* do the central characters possess striking good looks. Frances, Jane, and Lucy all improve considerably under the influence of love but are essentially plain; Rochester and M. Paul are ugly men; the Moores are handsome only to those who love them; Crimsworth, for all his aristocratic expression, is thin, short, and irregular of feature. Only the infatuated Zoraïde finds him 'beau comme Apollon quand il sourit de son air hautain'. [Chap. 20, II:83.] Even his son 'Victor is as little of a pretty child as I am of a handsome man, or his mother of a fine woman; he is pale and spare, with large eyes, as dark as those of Frances, and as deeply set as mine.' [Chap. 25, II:247.]

At least two critics have pointed out that Miss Brontë used phrenology as a kind of instant character analysis, depending upon the popular pseudo-science as a short cut to characterization.[1] Writing of one of his pupils, Crimsworth confirms her viciousness by phrenological reference: 'I wonder that any one, looking at that girl's head and countenance, would have received her under their roof. She had precisely the same shape of skull as Pope Alexander the Sixth; her organs of benevolence, veneration, conscientiousness, adhesiveness, were singularly small, those of self-esteem, firmness, destructiveness, combativeness, preposterously large.' [Chap. 12, I:198.]

Rather more interestingly, Miss Brontë used particular kinds of beauty as shorthand to character description, in the same way that she used phrenology. In *The Professor* she first introduced the three major categories of feminine beauty that she was to use to such effect in the later novels. When Crimsworth makes his entrance into the classroom at Mlle. Reuter's school, he encounters Eulalie, the prototype of such later figures as Georgiana Reed, Ginevra Fanshawe, and perhaps Dora Sykes. 'Eulalie was tall, and very finely shaped: she was fair, and her features were those of a Low-country Madonna; many a "figure de vierge" have I seen in Dutch pictures, exactly resembling hers; there were no angles in her shape or in her face, all was curve and roundness – neither thought, sentiment, nor passion, disturbed by line or flush the equality of her pale, clear skin; her noble bust heaved with her regular breathing, her eyes moved a little – by these evidences of life alone could I have distinguished her from some large handsome figure, moulded in wax.' [Chap. 10, I:164–5.] The overstuffed young ladies of this physical type Miss Brontë portrays as vain, silly, vacuous, and affected, but not vicious; occasionally, they are even affectionate after their own blowzy fashion.

The natural complement to these large, blonde women of

[1] Joe Lee Davis, intr. to *Jane Eyre* (Rinehart and Co., New York, 1950), pp. xv–xvi; and Wilfred M. Senseman, 'Charlotte Brontë's Use of Physiognomy and Phrenology,' *Papers of the Michigan Academy of Science, Arts, and Letters*, XXXVIII, 1953, pp. 475–86.

wax are the sensual, Oriental temptresses of the books: Crimsworth's pupil Caroline, Hunsden's mysterious Lucia, Blanche Ingram, the young Bertha Mason Rochester, and aspects of both Vashti and the painting of the 'gipsy-queen', Cleopatra.

Even among the pupils of Miss Brontë's schools, Caroline is outstanding. She has a pale olive complexion, black hair, and regular features. 'How, with the tintless pallor of her skin and the classic straightness of her lineaments, she managed to look sensual, I don't know. I think her lips and eyes contrived the affair between them, and the result left no uncertainty on the beholder's mind. She was sensual now, and in ten years' time she would be coarse—promise plain was written in her face of much future folly. . . .

'Caroline shook her loose ringlets of abundant but somewhat coarse hair over her rolling black eyes; parting her lips, as full as those of a hot-blooded Maroon, she showed her well-set teeth sparkling between them, and treated me at the same time to a smile "de sa façon". Beautiful as Pauline Borghese, she looked at the moment scarcely purer than Lucrèce de Borgia. Caroline was of noble family. I heard her lady-mother's character afterwards, and then I ceased to wonder at the precocious accomplishments of the daughter.' [Chap. 10, 1:165–7.]

Naturally, Pelet claims to be taken by the charms of Caroline: 'Ah there is beauty! beauty in perfection. What a cloud of sable curls about the face of a houri! What fascinating lips! What glorious black eyes! Your Byron would have worshipped her, and you—you cold frigid islander!—you played the austere, the insensible in the presence of an Aphrodite so exquisite?' [Chap. 11, 1:187.] Her very excess of sensuality, however, is Crimsworth's protection against her charms.

Bertha Mason Rochester is the perfection of Caroline's type: attractive when young, coarse a few years later, insane by middle age, so passionate as to lose all contact with reason and control, so sensual as to become nothing but an animal.

The third major group of beautiful women, with all the attendant defects of loveliness, is by far the most interesting of the lot, since they are the most credible, but they are also the most difficult to classify. Probably the epitome of the type is Pauline Home de Bassompierre. She is tiny, graceful, perfectly formed on an almost infantile scale, well bred, and with a charming, regular face; she is not unintelligent, and she is affectionate, but her lisp and the tininess of her figure are indicative of the immaturity of her mind and the shallowness of her emotions. Other examples of the type are Rosamond Oliver, Adèle, and, to a limited extent, Caroline Helstone. In *The Professor* the type has not yet completely emerged, but there are hints of it in Mrs. Edward Crimsworth, who is described as 'young, tall, and well shaped', with 'good animal spirits', 'a good complexion and features sufficiently marked but agreeable.' [Chap 1, 1:15–16.] Her insipidity is indicated by her voice: 'She spoke with a kind of lisp, not disagreeable, but childish. I soon saw also that there was a more than girlish–a somewhat infantine expression in her by no means small features; this lisp and expression were, I have no doubt, a charm in Edward's eyes, and would be so to those of most men, but they were not to mine. I sought her eye, desirous to read there the intelligence which I could not discern in her face or hear in her conversation; it was merry, rather small; by turns I saw vivacity, vanity, coquetry, look out through its irid, but I watched in vain for a glimpse of soul.' [Chap. 1, 1:16–17.] Mrs. Crimsworth is larger and less attractive than her sister-beauties, but the patent vacuity of her personality is not far removed from the basic frivolity of theirs.

In a somewhat more expected manner, great masculine beauty fares ill in Miss Brontë's works. The only two really handsome male characters of any importance are St. John Rivers and Dr. John. Rivers, with the beauty of classical Greece in his profile, is a narrow religious bigot, and Dr. John conceals commonplace emotions and a conventional mind behind his smiling, Celtic good looks.

Hunsden charges Crimsworth with finding the grapes of feminine beauty sour because he cannot reach them, but Crimsworth's repudiation of mere external attraction might stand directly for the attitude of the author: 'He could not be aware that . . . youth and loveliness had been to me every-day objects; that I had studied them at leisure and closely, and had seen the plain texture of truth under the embroidery of appearance.' [Chap. 22, II:128–9.]

Miss Brontë's first novel is probably her least overtly religious, but there is a strong feeling of the self-reliant Protestant ethic that so dominated her thinking. The preface to the book, with its renunciation of 'sudden turns' of fortune as a plot-agent, and with its insistence that the characters earn whatever happens to them, is consistent with the way in which Crimsworth as 'Adam's son' must learn the meaning of life before he can 'find so much as an arbour to sit down in'. The doctrine of self-reliance is given further statement within the novel in Frances' devoir about King Alfred. 'She had appreciated Alfred's courage under calamity, she had re-membered his Christian education, and had shown him, with the rooted confidence of those primitive days, relying on the scriptural Jehovah for aid against the mythological Destiny.' [Chap. 16, I:269–70.] On Christmas Eve Alfred defies the power of Fate: 'Pagan demon, I credit not thine omnipotence, and so cannot succumb to thy power. My God, whose Son, as on this night, took on Him the form of man, and for man vouchsafed to suffer and bleed, controls thy hand, and without His behest thou canst not strike a stroke. My God is sinless, eternal, all-wise—in Him is my trust; and though stripped and crushed by thee—though naked, desolate, void of resource—I do not despair, I cannot despair: were the lance of Guthrum now wet with my blood, I should not despair. I watch, I toil, I hope, I pray; Jehovah, in his own time, will aid.' [Chap. 16, I:268–9.] It is worth stressing here the denial of the power of Fate because an understanding of Miss Brontë's position is important in seeing that the otherwise incredible

coincidences of such a book as *Jane Eyre* are neither viola-
tions of spiritual probability nor the workings of blind Fate,
but the material manifestations of a world order run by
Divine will co-operating with man's own will. To put the
matter more simply, the man who accepts Providential
guidance, and so helps to shape his own world, will find that
events and circumstances do not run counter to his own
nature.

The roots of Charlotte Brontë's religious faith are not far
to seek, of course, since she was the daughter of a clergyman
and lived most of her life under his roof, next the parish
church. Unlike Emily, whose religion seems to have had
pantheistic beliefs added to Christian doctrine, Charlotte
Brontë seldom varied far from the conventional Evangelical
position of her father, who had been educated at Cambridge
when that University was the stronghold of Evangelicalism.
Mrs. Brontë had been brought up as a Methodist, but she
settled comfortably into being the wife of an Anglican priest,
and Haworth Parsonage, although friendly to Non-Confor-
mists, seems never to have been infected with the enthusiasm
that was the chief distinguishing mark of Methodism at the
time.

Mr. Brontë, in looking for a curate, once wrote to describe
his own theological position that set the tone for Haworth
Parsonage: 'As far as I know myself, I think I may venture to
say that I am no Bigot. Yet I could not feel comfortable with
a coadjutor who would deem it his duty to preach the appal-
ling doctrines of personal Election and Reprobation. As I
should consider these decidedly derogatory to the Attributes
of God, so also I should be fearful of evil consequence to the
hearers from the enforcement of final perseverance as an
essential article of belief.' [Shorter, ii:422.] Mr. Brontë was
as hostile to extreme High Church practices and Roman
Catholicism as he was to extreme Calvinistic doctrines. On
one occasion he spoke of a liturgical Anglican service as
'idle and ostentatious pageantry got up in the church, where

the Gospel was once faithfully preached.' [Shorter, ii:405.]
He was opposed to Roman Catholic emancipation and probably as bigoted about Roman Catholicism as his daughter
Charlotte, if we can judge from the tone of the letters that
passed between them when she was in Brussels.

'Whatever such critics as he of the *Mirror* may say,' Miss
Brontë wrote to W. S. Williams in 1847, 'I love the Church of
England. Her ministers, indeed, I do not regard as infallible
personages. I have seen too much of them for that, but to the
Establishment, with all her faults—the profane Athanasian
creed *ex*cluded—I am sincerely attached.' [Shorter, i:377.]

The assurance of the general rightness of the Establishment
and the sense of fellowship within its fold were never enough
for Miss Brontë, nor was the austere relationship of man
with his Maker of much comfort, for she constantly felt the
terrible need of closer intimacy with another human being, so
that her daily life could be some reflection of her faith. In a
moving letter in 1837 she had written to Ellen Nussey, wishing that they might live together in Christian fellowship.
That her real need was for a husband, a need that she faces
directly in the lives of her heroines, if not in her own, only
makes the letter the more touching. 'If I could always live
with you, and daily read the Bible with you—if your lips and
mine could at the same time drink the same draught, from
the same pure fountain of mercy—I hope, I trust, I might one
day become better, far better than my evil, wandering
thoughts, my corrupt heart, cold to the spirit and warm to the
flesh, will now permit me to be. I often plan the pleasant life
which we might lead together, strengthening each other in
that power of self-denial, that hallowed and glowing devotion, which the first saints of God often attained to. My eyes
fill with tears when I contrast the bliss of such a state,
brightened by hopes of the future, with the melancholy state
I now live in, uncertain that I ever felt true contrition, wandering in thought and deed, longing for holiness, which I
shall *never, never* obtain, smitten at times to the heart with the

conviction that ghastly Calvinistic doctrines are true—darkened, in short, by the very shadows of spiritual death. If Christian perfection be necessary to salvation, I shall never be saved; my heart is a very hot-bed for sinful thoughts, and when I decide on an action I scarcely remember to look to my Redeemer for direction. I know not how to pray; I cannot bend my life to the grand end of doing good; I go on constantly seeking my own pleasure, pursuing the gratification of my own desires, I forget God, and will not God forget me? And, meantime, I know the greatness of Jehovah; I acknowledge the perfection of His word; I adore the purity of the Christian faith; my theory is right, my practice horribly wrong.' [Gaskell, Chap. 8, 1:177–8.]

With two notable exceptions, Miss Brontë was probably as tolerant of other forms of Christianity as most of her contemporaries were. Her treatment of the two exceptions is one of the least attractive aspects of her writing, both because it reveals a stubborn intolerance and because the strength of that intolerance flashes out in *The Professor* to help ruin the unity of the novel. The light that 'falls on earth from Heaven', she wrote, the rays of truth that 'pierce the darkness of this life and world' are so 'few, faint, and scattered', that one ought to ask who 'without presumption can assert that he has found the *only* true path upwards?' [Shorter, 1:443–4.] Who, that is, except the most 'enthusiastic' of Dissenters, and Roman Catholics?

Dissent she distrusted because it allowed the reason to be perverted by undisciplined emotionalism, so that the revelling in emotion became an end in itself. Some evidence of the detached curiosity Miss Brontë felt about the emotional excesses of her fellow-Christians is indicated by her letter to Ellen Nussey, hoping to go to a 'Ranters' meeting-house' at Easton to see 'What they were up to.' [*SHB*, 1:190.] Among the works to which Caroline Helstone has access are 'some mad Methodist Magazines, full of miracles and apparitions, of preternatural warnings, ominous dreams, and frenzied fanaticism.' [*Shirley*, Chap. 22, ii:269.] The malice and hatred displayed by the Dissenters in *Shirley* indicate how little Miss Brontë thought that their religion could improve their morals. In *The Professor* Edward Crimsworth, baffled by his brother's quiet religious belief, sends as his spy ' "a joined Methodist", which did not (be it understood) prevent him from being at the same time an engrained rascal'. [Chap. 3, i:37.] In general, as one would expect from the daughter of a Methodist, Miss Brontë tried to be as tolerant as possible of Dissenters who were sincere in their beliefs; the three curates in *Shirley*, so conscious of their own superiority as members of the Established Church, are a direct transcription of the curates near Haworth whom she so surprisingly rebuked sharply for 'glorifying themselves and abusing Dissenters'. [Shorter, i:301.] As a good Evangelical, she liked neither Dissenters nor High Churchmen, but even more she disliked their reviling of each other.

On the subject of Roman Catholicism, Miss Brontë was quite as unfair as the curates were on Dissent. To account completely for her aversion to that church would be to rewrite the history of nineteenth-century England, as well as to investigate every disappointment she felt in Brussels. The main reason, however, that she acknowledged (perhaps quite a different thing from the real reason) for this hatred was the old Protestant *canard* that the Roman Catholic by submitting his sins to confession and forgiveness is giving up his own responsibility and conscience into the hands of another, and that he therefore has no control—and, indeed, need have no control—over his own actions.

In one of her heavily ironic letters to George Smith, Miss Brontë wrote that Wiseman's having become Archbishop of Westminster led her to think that all Cornhill must become Catholic: 'What if that presumptuous self-reliance, that audacious championship of Reason and Common Sense which ought to have been crushed out of you all in your cradles, or at least during your school days, and which, perhaps, on the contrary, were encouraged and developed, what if those things should induce you madly to oppose the returning supremacy and advancing victory of the Holy Catholic Church?' [*SHB*, iii:176.]

One of the most threatening aspects of Roman Catholicism is that it is inculcated so early. Zoraïde Reuter is, of course, far past the age when she might be rescued, and even the girls in her establishment have already been hardened in their immodesty and impropriety: 'I know nothing of the arcana of the Roman Catholic religion, and I am not a bigot in matters of theology, but I suspect the root of this precocious impurity, so obvious, so general in Popish countries [Miss Brontë had seen but one], is to be found in the discipline, if not the doctrines of the Church of Rome. I record what I have seen: these girls belonged to what are called the respectable ranks of society; they had all been carefully brought up, yet was the mass of them mentally depraved.' [Chap. 12, i:193.]

Miss Brontë's hatred of Roman Catholicism existed side-by-side with a partial attraction towards it. In Brussels she attended Roman Catholic services, and on one occasion even attempted to go to confession, an incident she used with great effect in *Villette*. In 1851 she wrote from London to tell of the two great theatrical experiences she had had, the performance of Rachel and the equally dramatic confirmation at which Cardinal Wiseman officiated. One wonders if their conjunction in the same paragraph of the letter does not indicate that she felt for both of them a mixed attraction and repulsion. 'On Sunday I went to the Spanish Ambassador's Chapel, where Cardinal Wiseman, in his archiepiscopal robes and mitre, held a confirmation. The whole scene was impiously theatrical.' [Gaskell, Chap. 23, ii:216–17.] In her letter to her father describing the same event, she significantly associated her disapproval of Wiseman with her dislike of Methodist excesses; she noted his 'quadruple chin . . . a very large mouth with oily lips'. He spoke 'in a smooth whining manner, just like a canting Methodist preacher'. [Shorter, II:219–20.]

Concisely she indicated in a letter from Brussels her feelings about Rome: 'People talk of the danger which Protestants expose themselves to, in going to reside in Catholic countries, and thereby running the chance of changing their faith. My advice to all Protestants who are tempted to do anything so besotted as turn Catholics is, to walk over the sea on to the Continent; to attend mass sedulously for a time; to note well the mummeries thereof; also the idiotic, mercenary aspect of all the priests; and *then*, if they are still disposed to consider Papistry in any other light than a most feeble, childish piece of humbug, let them turn Papists at once – that's all. I consider Methodism, Quakerism, and the extremes of High and Low Churchism foolish, but Roman Catholicism beats them all. At the same time, allow me to tell you, that there are some Catholics who are as good as any Christians can be to whom the Bible is a sealed book, and much better than many Protestants.' [Gaskell, Chap. 11, I:268.]

In *The Professor* all Miss Brontë's spleen against Roman Catholics is plain, but it remains unintegrated into the themes of the book, except as it equates Crimsworth's sensual attraction to Zoraïde with her moral inadequacies caused by her religion, and it shows the enfeeblement of the reason and the will in the pallid little Sylvie. In *Villette* the whole background of the corrupting influence of the Church is made part of the fabric of the story; in the first novel it remains an unattractive excrescence.

Charlotte Brontë was not unaware of her own failings, and of the reasons for them, but the strength of her convictions sometimes blinded her into feeling that art and truth were in necessary opposition. 'The first duty of an author is, I conceive, a faithful allegiance to Truth and Nature,' she wrote to Williams in 1848; 'his second, such a conscientious study of Art as shall enable him to interpret eloquently and effectively the oracles delivered by those two great deities. The Bells are very sincere in their worship of Truth, and they hope to apply themselves to the consideration of Art, so as to attain one day the power of speaking the language of conviction in the accents of persuasion; though they rather apprehend that whatever pains they take to modify and soften, an abrupt word or vehement tone will now and then occur to startle ears polite, whenever the subject shall chance to be such as moves their spirits within them.' [Shorter, 1:445.] In her second novel Charlotte Brontë managed to combine the stern dictates of what she thought of as Truth and the persuasive subtleties of Art into one of the masterpieces of the English novel.

2

JANE EYRE

'Novelists should never allow themselves to weary of the study of real life,' wrote Charlotte Brontë with sweet reasonableness in *The Professor*. Then, rather less convincingly: 'If they observed this duty conscientiously, they would give us fewer pictures chequered with vivid contrasts of light and shade; they would seldom elevate their heroes and heroines to the heights of rapture–still seldomer sink them to the depths of despair; for if we rarely taste the fulness of joy in this life, we yet more rarely savour the acrid bitterness of hopeless anguish.' [Chap. 19, ii:28.] In short, such conscientious novelists would not write *Jane Eyre*.

The primary impression of Miss Brontë's first masterpiece is of anguished torment and nearly intolerable happiness. Because she believed that life's joys are few beside its sorrows (whatever she may have written in the person of Crimsworth), the reader's strongest recollection is probably of the blinding fierceness of the rebellion of Jane's lonely heart against the loveless tyranny of Gateshead, the pangs of her physical and emotional hunger at Lowood, the aching frustration of her first love of Rochester, the death-in-life of her discovery that he is already married, the solitary agony of her night on the moor, her merciless grinding under the juggernaut of St. John's ambitious piety. The fitful ecstasy of Jane's joy is made brighter by being thrown in relief against her trials and by the rareness of its visitation: the lyrical garden scene when Rochester pours out his love against a counterpoint of the nightingale's song; the night when he swoops her into his saddle before him like a demon lover enveloping her in his cloak; the muted, autumnal delicacy of their reconciliation at Ferndean, poised between laughter and tears.

The play of Charlotte Brontë's imagination achieves many of its finest effects by lurid contrasts of illumination and shade, by the relentless light of rational day set against the menacing shadows of dead of night ('ever the hour of fatality at Thornfield'), by the juxtaposition of pinafores and supernatural flashes of light, burnt porridge and raging epidemic, schoolroom doldrums and the long, terrible laughter of Grace Poole—or is it the lunatic mirth of Bertha?—housecleaning and a universe shaken by supernatural convulsions: the counterpoise of a world of mundane detail and the world of Gothic imagination. It is a witch's broth of ingredients, but for the first time Charlotte Brontë has the imaginative, comprehensive grasp of her material that manages to fuse its disparate parts into a real unity, one probably owing more to the singleness of her vision than it does to her formal considerations of the problems of structure in the novel. Whether the pattern she achieved was a completely deliberate and rational one, or whether it sprang from somewhere beneath the surface of her consciousness is ultimately unimportant. The heart has its forms, as well as its reasons, that the reason knows nothing of. The novel is improbable in the sense that all cosmic and supernatural action is improbable, even when it seems inevitable. It is larger than life because it is Miss Brontë's vision of the totality of life, of man's relation to his heart, mind, loved ones, and God, and any such vision must necessarily transcend the probable limits of experience of any individual.

In *Jane Eyre* the movement of the action is towards the maturity and self-knowledge of its two central characters. Jane's maturation is, of course, the more detailed and central of the two, but Rochester's growth is necessary to complete Miss Brontë's vision of the world. Jane is kept by conscience

and the force of example from making gross errors of judgment, but Rochester's story is of sin and redemption; the
prudent and the imprudent inhabit the same world. The
result is not to divide the novel but to intensify it by showing
parallel although differing actions, an effect like that which
Shakespeare achieves by doubling his plots, so that, for example, Gloucester's trials illuminate those of Lear.

The central consciousness of the novel, however, is completely single, that of Jane alone, so that one sees all the
action and characters through her eyes. This is in part, of
course, a result of the first-person narration of the novel, but
even more the result of Jane's reactions being the centre of
interest when she is with others. Even when she is the apparently passive recipient of information from other characters,
we never forget what Jane is feeling. When, for example,
Rochester is telling her of his trio of Continental mistresses,
we are less absorbed with his narration and his own feelings
of remorse than we are with Jane's reactions to the necessary
finitude of relationships based on passion alone. To put the
matter another way, the narrative of the mistresses is really
important at this point only so far as it relates to Jane, and we
feel no shock that she takes it as an object lesson to herself,
when, instead of worrying about Rochester's excesses, she says
to his protestation of remorse over past dissipation: 'I felt
the truth of these words; and I drew from them the certain
inference, that if I were so far to forget myself and all the
teaching that had ever been instilled into me, as—under any
pretext—with any justification—through any temptation—to
become the successor of these poor girls, he would one day
regard me with the same feeling which now in his mind
desecrated their memory.' [Chap. 27, III:29-30.]

Since we are taken so far into Jane's mind, and since we
find it an honest and likable one, we trust her reactions rather
than peering over her shoulder in order to form our own
opinions. In short, she seems a reliable observer. However,
the story is told by Jane as a mature woman after an interval

of ten years from the main action, and we are occasionally reminded that the narrator is no longer the ingenuous girl of the story, as when she says of herself sitting on the causeway when Rochester first rides into the story on his tall horse: 'In those days I was young, and all sorts of fancies bright and dark tenanted my mind: the memories of nursery stories were there amongst other rubbish; and when they recurred, maturing youth added to them a vigour and vividness beyond what childhood could give.' [Chap. 12, 1:212.] The effect of the mature Jane's view of her girlhood is not to discount the young Jane as a narrator but to remind us that her reactions are those of a partially unformed mind. The much-criticized accounts of 'society' when the Ingrams and their party invade Thornfield perhaps owe less to Miss Brontë's lack of experience in such company than they do to the deliberate intention of making the account of their doings seem the reporting of Jane's maturity remembering her jejune reactions to a society that despises and excludes her. Miss Brontë's own humiliations as a governess have been objectified and exorcized. Blanche Ingram's immortal words of reproof to the footman, 'Cease that chatter, blockhead! and do my bidding,' quite properly tell us more of the young Jane's stereotyped and immature reaction to 'haughty beauty' than they do of the character and speech habits of the relatively unimportant Blanche.

The setting of the story is carefully divided into five distinct locales, each of which has its particular significance in Jane's history, and each of which is like an act in a five-act drama. Her early childhood is spent in Gateshead Hall, the home of the Reeds; from there she goes to Lowood, where she comes under the influence of Mr. Brocklehurst, Miss Temple, and Helen Burns; as governess to Adèle at Thornfield she falls in love with Rochester; after the discovery of the existence of Bertha, Jane runs away and is taken into Moor House, the home of her cousins, the Rivers family; in the conclusion of the book she and Rochester are united at his crumbling hunting-lodge, Ferndean Manor. There are, in addition, two scenes in which Jane returns to an earlier home to discover changes in both herself and those she has known in the past: from Thornfield she returns to the deathbed of Mrs. Reed at Gateshead, and from Moor House she returns to Thornfield to find only its blind windows and gaping walls. Miss Brontë carefully emphasizes that each new habitation is to be a new stage in Jane's life, by an *entr'acte*, a detailed description of the journey, with Jane looking forward to each new locale with a mixture of pleasure and dread, trying to discover what the change may mean to her. 'It is a very strange sensation to inexperienced youth to feel itself quite alone in the world: cut adrift from every connection; uncertain whether the port to which it is bound can be reached, and prevented by many impediments from returning to that it has quitted.' [Chap. 11, 1:172.] Each journey is undertaken in loneliness, each new habitation except the last brings Jane into the orbit of new and unexpected friends; however solitary one's way appears in the world, Miss Brontë seems to say, it is warmed by one's fellow creatures. After arrival Jane describes each setting as carefully as if it were the scenery for a further act in a drama of her life.

On her last night in Lowood Jane is unable to sleep, conscious that 'a phase of my life was closing to-night, a new one opening to-morrow'. [Chap. 10, 1:165.] Her clearly dramatic intent Miss Brontë makes overt at the beginning of the next chapter, the opening of the Thornfield section: 'A new chapter in a novel is something like a new scene in a play; and when I draw up the curtain this time, reader, you must fancy you see a room in the George Inn at Millcote.' [Chap. 11, 1:171.]

The dominant tone of the Gateshead section is that of passion, sensuality, emotion, superstition, and the other manifestations of the non-rational aspects of man's nature. Mrs. Reed, whose capricious spoiling of her children parallels her cold dislike of Jane, rules the house, setting the tone

of self-indulgence that pervades it. Her son, given up to precocious dissipation and vicious cruelty, bullies Jane, as do his
sisters, the spoiled, petted, golden-curled Georgiana, and
the 'headstrong and selfish' Eliza, mistress of that coldest of
vices, avarice. The family pattern of one brother and two
sisters is to be repeated later in the book with the Ingrams
and the Rivers family; here the contrast is between the various
kinds of self-indulgence within one family: John's violence,
Eliza's calculation, and Georgiana's indolence.

With no standard by which to guide her conduct save that
which surrounds her, Jane naturally becomes as passionately
self-willed as the Reeds themselves, in an attempt to win at
least respect, if not love, from those who bully her. 'Did ever
anybody see such a picture of passion?' [Chap. 1, 1:10] asks
Mrs. Reed's maid when John is saved from the avenging
fury Jane. 'If you become passionate and rude, Missis will
send you away, I am sure,' [Chap. 2, 1:13] Bessie warns
Jane. And it is on the note of her violent denunciation of
Mrs. Reed that Jane eventually leaves Gateshead for the
first time. For all of our own and Miss Brontë's sympathy for
Jane's heartbreak, it is clear that she is something of a brat,
even if the fault is not her own. The self-infecting quality of
passion—and the terrible letdown of its aftermath—is indicated by Jane after her tongue-lashing of her aunt: 'Something of vengeance I had tasted for the first time; as aro-
matic wine it seemed on swallowing, warm and racy: its
after-flavour, metallic and corroding, gave me a sensation as
if I had been poisoned. Willingly would I now have gone and
asked Mrs. Reed's pardon; but I knew, partly from experience and partly from instinct, that was the way to make her
repulse me with double scorn, thereby re-exciting every
turbulent impulse of my nature.' [Chap. 4, 1:62.] In a meta-
phor that is more significant for the book as a whole, Jane
indicates the same idea in terms of fire and ashes: 'A ridge of
lighted heath, alive, glancing, devouring, would have been a
meet emblem of my mind when I accused and menaced Mrs.

Reed: the same ridge, black and blasted after the flames are
dead, would have represented as metely my subsequent condition, when half an hour's silence and reflection had shewn
me the madness of my conduct, and the dreariness of my
hated and hating position.' [Chap. 4 1:62.] Fire throughout
the book is occasionally associated in a naturally symbolic
way with comfort and love, the normal feelings of the healthy
personality before the hearth, but as that fire on the hearth
may become dangerous when it is out of control, so the undisciplined emotions become threatening, and raging flame
takes on the aspect of devastation of unleashed and self-
consuming passion as Bertha Rochester wanders through the
house with her candle, setting fire to her husband's bed, and
finally starting the flaming destruction that culminates in her
own death, Rochester's maiming, and the ruin of Thornfield.
The very nursery fire, kindled as a comfort to Jane in her illness after her experiences in the red room, takes on the
terrors of hell in her disturbed state: 'The next thing I remember is waking up with a feeling as if I had had a frightful
night-mare, and seeing before me a terrible red glare, crossed
with thick black bars. I heard voices, too, speaking with a
hollow sound, and as if muffled by a rush of wind or water:
agitation, uncertainty, and an all predominating sense of
terror confused my faculties. . . . In five minutes more, the
cloud of bewilderment dissolved: I knew quite well that I
was in my own bed, and that the red glare was the nursery
fire.' [Chap. 3, 1:24.]

Some measure of Miss Brontë's religious position in the
novel is indicated by Jane's thinking of hell only when her
mind is confused. When Mr. Brocklehurst attempts to
frighten her with his visions of hell as a pit full of fire, a lake
burning with brimstone, and asks Jane how to avoid it, she
answers with the sturdy good sense that characterizes her
later in the book: 'I must keep in good health, and not die.'
[Chap. 4, 1:52.] The answer is meant as a childish defeat of
Mr. Brocklehurst's narrow theology, but it might stand as

Miss Brontë's general position that man's hell and heaven are sufficient on earth without looking unnecessarily for them elsewhere. Religion is essential, but it is largely concerned with man's position in this world.

Jane's association of the nursery fire with hell is a reflection of her experiences in the red room, where she is thrust as punishment for her defence against the attack of John Reed. Here, as elsewhere, the colour red becomes connected naturally with passion and the non-rational. Her normal terror in the bedroom of her dead uncle is strengthened by her own susperstitions and predispositions to believe in the unnatural quality of each noise and of any movement such as that of the ray of light that traverses the wall: 'I can now conjecture readily that this streak of light was, in all likelihood, a gleam from a lantern, carried by some one across the lawn; but then, prepared as my mind was for horror, shaken as my nerves were by agitation, I thought the swift-darting beam was a herald of some coming vision from another world.' [Chap. 2, 1:21.] Throughout the book, the pattern of Jane's perceptions is of this order, initially to assign non-rational origins to phenomena that she cannot otherwise explain, and then, as she grows in understanding, to give more rational explanations for them. The point is made about emotional phenomena as well as physical. While she is suffering in the red room, she ponders on why she is unloved and mistreated: 'I could not answer the ceaseless inward question—*why* I thus suffered: now, at the distance of—I will not say how many years, I see it clearly.

'I was a discord in Gateshead Hall: I was like nobody there: I had nothing in harmony with Mrs. Reed or her children, or her chosen vassalage. If they did not love me, in fact, as little did I love them. They were not bound to regard with affection a thing that could not sympathize with one amongst them; a heterogeneous thing, opposed to them in temperament, in capacity, in propensities; a useless thing, incapable of serving their interest, or adding to their pleasure;

a noxious thing, cherishing the germs of indignation at their treatment, of contempt of their judgment.' [Chap. 2, 1:18–19.] Miss Brontë throughout the Gateshead section of the novel achieves a marvellous balance between the sympathy that she draws from her reader for the lonely child, and the more sober judgment of the mature Jane, that as a child she brought much of her punishment upon herself. Nowhere does she achieve this balance more delicately than in the terrible vigil in the red room, where Jane twice looks at herself in the looking-glass, and with her self-absorbed gaze on her own sorrow finds that 'all looked colder and darker in that visionary hollow than in reality; and the strange little figure there gazing at me, with a white face and arms specking the gloom, and glittering eyes of fear moving where all else was still, had the effect of a real spirit: I thought it like one of the tiny phantoms, half fairy, half imp, Bessie's evening stories represented as coming up out of lone, ferny dells in moors, and appearing before the eyes of belated travellers.' [Chap, 2, 1:16.]

As one would expect from a child still living in the realms of the non-rational, Jane stuffs her head with stories of fairyland and the landscapes of Lilliput and Brobdingnag, 'the little fields, houses, and trees, the diminutive people, the tiny cows, sheep, and birds of the one realm; and the corn-fields forest-high, the mighty mastiffs, the monster cats, the tower-like men and women, of the other.' [Chap. 3, 1:29.] Her happiest moments are when Bessie tells her fairy tales and sings her ballads, or when she is alone and takes refuge from the world by sitting 'cross-legged, like a Turk' in the window seat of the breakfast room, shut off by the red moreen curtain from the hatred of the Reeds on one side, and on the other 'the clear panes of glass, protecting, but not separating me from the drear November day'. [Chap. 1, 1:3.] There, insulated from the world of reality, she can turn over the pages of Bewick's *History of British Birds*, ignoring most of the letterpress and allowing herself to drift into romantic reveries inspired by the pictures. So far, the arts of literature and painting are used not to discover truth but to obscure it, acting as tools of the idle fancy rather than of the fully engaged Imagination. Even Bessie's ballad of the orphan child, with its burden of the comfort of God for the homeless becomes 'a really doleful' song. ' "Come, Miss Jane, don't cry," said Bessie, as she finished. She might as well have said to the fire, "don't burn!" but how could she divine the morbid suffering to which I was a prey?'[1] [Chap. 3, 1:31.]

At Gateshead there has been little mention of religion, the force that is to be the main influence on Jane when she goes to Lowood. What religion there has been has served only to colour her childish thoughts with the charnel horrors of the vault under the chancel of Gateshead Church and to feed her already inflamed appetite for romance with the more exciting aspects of 'Revelations, and the book of Daniel, and Genesis and Samuel, and a little bit of Exodus, and some parts of Kings and Chronicles, and Job and Jonah'. [Chap. 4, 1:52–3.]

At Lowood School the presiding genius is Mr. Brocklehurst, the manager and treasurer of the establishment, but it is not his influence that stays with Jane in later life, for she reacts against him at their first meeting, while she is still at Gateshead. As she enters the breakfast room, she looks 'up at –a black pillar!–such, at least, appeared to me, at first sight, the straight, narrow, sable-clad shape standing erect on the rug: the grim face at the top was like a carved mask, placed above the shaft by way of capital.' [Chap. 4, 1:50.] To characterize Mr. Brocklehurst, Miss Brontë uses one of the many literary parallels that she scatters throughout the book. Jane, who has been used to reading *Gulliver's Travels*, reacts to the innate coarseness in Brocklehurst as Gulliver does when he is brought close to the offensive bodies and faces of the 'tower-like' Brobdingnagians. 'I stepped across the rug;

[1] The ballad, incidentally, like so many other details in the novel, becomes a foreshadowing of Jane's agonies on the marshes and moors, where she, like the singer of the song, is to fear the 'grey rocks' and the 'false lights' before she can accept that she is protected by Providence.

he placed me square and straight before him. What a face he had, now that it was almost on a level with mine! what a great nose! and what a mouth! and what large prominent teeth!'[1] [Chap. 4, 1:51.] The grossness of Mr. Brocklehurst's soul is reflected in the repulsiveness of his face.

His treatment of his pupils is indicated by his satisfaction in having 'studied how best to mortify in them the worldly sentiment of pride'. [Chap. 4, 1:55.] 'Plain fare, simple attire, unsophisticated accommodations' are the attributes he claims for his school, but they are euphemisms for starvation, inadequate clothing, and freezing quarters.

In contrast to the physical comforts of Gateshead, Lowood has only scant food that scarcely keeps the young girls alive and equally meagre doctrines that fail to nourish their souls. Everywhere there is intolerable cold, freezing the water in the wash basins, covering unbooted feet and ungloved hands with chilblains, a physical parallel to the spiritual and emotional frigidity of the school. There are few passages in English literature, aside from the description of the bedesman in Keats's 'Eve of St. Agnes', where the sheer agony of physical cold is so vividly recreated as in the descriptions of Lowood. The coldness of Brocklebridge Church and the numbing qualities of the ministrations of Mr. Brocklehurst, that columnar man of cold black marble, are made patent in the discomforts of the little girls: 'We set out cold, we arrived at church colder; during the morning service we became almost paralysed. It was too far to return to dinner, and an allowance of cold meat and bread, in the same penurious proportion observed in our ordinary meals, was served round between the services.

'At the close of the afternoon service we returned by an exposed and hilly road, where the bitter winter wind, blowing over a range of snowy summits to the north, almost flayed the skin from our faces.' [Chap. 7, 1:106–7.] Even on

[1] The Brocklehurst-Brobdingnagian comparison is repeated in the school-room scene, Chap. 7, 1:109, 117.

the return to the school there is no room for the younger children by the fire, and they are forced to huddle together for warmth, 'wrapping their starved arms in their pinafores'.

The only moments of real physical warmth at Lowood occur when Miss Temple offers Jane and Helen tea and sympathy before her own hospitable hearth—one suspects that the seed-cake is as important as the affection—and when the girls are freed by the epidemic to run barefoot through the woods in the summer sun, unchained from the chilling routine of the school.

The unnatural quality of Mr. Brocklehurst's religion and precepts is pointed up by his reaction to the red curls of one of the pupils whom he sees on his tour of inspection: ' "Why, in defiance of every precept and principle of this house, does she conform to the world so openly – here in an evangelical, charitable establishment—as to wear her hair one mass of curls?"

' "Julia's hair curls naturally," returned Miss Temple, still more quietly.

' "Naturally! Yes, but we are not to conform to nature: I wish these girls to be the children of Grace." ' [Chap. 7, 1:113.] In this novel, as well as in her others, Miss Brontë treats extreme Evangelicalism and Calvinism[1] with contempt no more veiled than Miss Temple's righteous anger at Brocklehurst for starving her pupils.

Helen Burns is Jane's teacher in one of the major lessons that the younger girl must learn, that of patience. Jane carries with her from Gateshead the exhilarating sense of victory that she has achieved over John Reed and his mother by turning on them in anger, and, even at the cost of the inevitable aftermath of retaliation, it becomes her pattern for dealing with injustice. 'If people were always kind and obedient to those who are cruel and unjust,' she tells Helen, 'the

---

[1] Mrs. Kathleen Tillotson points out the Calvinistic aspects of Brocklehurst and Rivers set in contrast to the Arminianism of Helen Burns's religion, *Novels of the Eighteen-Forties* (Clarendon Press, Oxford, 1954), n., pp. 310–11.

wicked people would have it all their own way: they would never feel afraid, and so they would never alter, but would grow worse and worse. When we are struck at without a reason, we should strike back again very hard; I am sure we should—so hard as to teach the person who struck us never to do it again. . . . But I feel this, Helen: I must dislike those who, whatever I do to please them, persist in disliking me; I must resist those who punish me unjustly. It is as natural as that I should love those who show me affection, or submit to punishment when I feel it is deserved.'

To Jane's outburst Helen replies in her usual mild way: 'Heathens and savage tribes hold that doctrine, but Christians and civilised nations disown it. . . . It is not violence that best overcomes hate—nor vengeance that most certainly heals injury. . . . Read the New Testament, and observe what Christ says, and how he acts—make his word your rule, and his conduct your example. . . . Love your enemies; bless them that curse you; do good to them that hate you and despitefully use you.' [Chap. 6, 1:101-2.] Helen's persuasiveness is shown when Jane, 'mindful of Helen's warnings against the indulgence of resentment', tells Miss Temple of her childhood at Gateshead and puts 'into the narrative far less gall and wormwood than ordinarily'. [Chap. 8, 1:128.]

Helen's counsel is of perfection, but it would scarcely equip even the most unvindictive of mankind, let alone Jane, for living in this world. Jane loves Helen and strives to emulate her, but her real model is the fittingly named Miss Temple, who can rebel against evil authority when the welfare of others is at stake. Jane's last act of rebellion at Lowood is far different in character from that prompted by pride and personal injury. When Helen has a pasteboard bearing the word 'Slattern' unjustly bound around her 'large, mild, intelligent, and benign-looking forehead', Jane tears it off and throws it into the fire in an outburst of generous indignation: 'the fury of which she was incapable had been burning in my soul all day, and tears, hot and large, had continually been scalding my cheek; for the spectacle of her sad resignation gave me an intolerable pain at the heart.' [Chap. 8, 1:133–4.] To the end of the book Jane is incapable of calmly suffering injustice to others.

From Helen, Jane also learns to restrain her passionate need of love and to endure loneliness with a Christian Stoicism: 'I cannot bear to be solitary and hated, Helen,' she tells her friend. 'Look here; to gain some real affection from you, or Miss Temple, or any other whom I truly love, I would willingly submit to have the bone of my arm broken, or to let a bull toss me, or to stand behind a kicking horse, and let it dash its hoof at my chest,–'.

But Helen urges the moderation and endurance that Jane is to need in her long troubles before marriage: 'Hush, Jane! you think too much of the love of human beings; you are too impulsive, too vehement: the sovereign hand that created your frame, and put life into it, has provided you with other resources than your feeble self, or than creatures feeble as you. Besides this earth, and besides the race of men, there is an invisible world and a kingdom of spirits: that world is round us, for it is everywhere; and those spirits watch us, for they are commissioned to guard us; . . . God waits only the separation of spirit from flesh to crown us with a full reward. Why, then, should we ever sink overwhelmed with distress, when life is soon over, and death is so certain an entrance to happiness: to glory?' [Chap. 8, 1:124–6.]

As Jane's character at Gateshead has been shown by her reading habits, so Helen is economically characterized by her introduction bent over a copy of *Rasselas*, with its theme of philosophical acceptance. Jane asks to see the book: 'a brief examination convinced me that the contents were less taking than the title: "Rasselas" looked dull to my trifling taste; I saw nothing about fairies, nothing about genii; no bright variety seemed spread over the closely printed pages.' [Chap. 5, 1:85.]

The dual lesson of patience under apparent injustice, and

the wholesome distrust of too much reliance upon human affections is necessary for Jane, so that she will later not fall into the same moral trap as Rochester, who reacts against his own injuries by formulating a completely individual and relative morality without reference to universal moral law. Her own experiences at Gateshead and the precepts of Helen at Lowood have taught Jane that the aftermath of flouting moral law is bitter.

Despite its necessity to Jane, Helen's advice is of a faultlessness that fallible man can scarcely hope to emulate. Unlike Brocklehurst, who is not good enough for this world, Helen is too good for it. Unable to cope with mundane life, she recognizes in her death a release from an existence for which she is not equipped: 'By dying young I shall escape great sufferings. I had not qualities or talents to make my way very well in the world: I should have been continually at fault.' [Chap. 9, 1:148.] For all that she has taught Jane, she can only counsel saintliness, not how to deal with the world of men. Helen's religion is far more attractive than that of St. John Rivers, but in their dual denial of the need of human love, both neglect the normal and spontaneous promptings of the generous heart.

The smell of death around her causes Jane to make her 'first earnest effort to comprehend what had been infused [into her mind] concerning heaven and hell: and for the first time it recoiled, baffled; and for the first time, glancing behind, on each side, and before it, it saw all round an unfathomed gulf: it felt the one point where it stood—the present; all the rest was formless cloud and vacant depth; and it shuddered at the thought of tottering, and plunging amid that chaos.' [Chap. 9, 1:144.] No wonder that Jane asks at her friend's pious death: 'Where is God? What is God?' and ponders on heaven: 'Where is that region? Does it exist?' [Chap. 9, 1:148–9.] A religion whose terms of reference are totally unearthly has little relevance for Jane.

Significantly, it is not Helen but Miss Temple who is to be

the major influence on Jane, for she is of this world, with the more normal affections indicated by marriage to her excellent Rev. Mr. Nasmyth. 'I had imbibed from her something of her nature and much of her habits,' writes Jane; 'more harmonious thoughts; what seemed better regulated feelings had become the inmates of my mind. I had given in allegiance to duty and order; I was quiet; I believed I was content: to the eyes of others, usually even to my own, I appeared a disciplined and subdued character.' [Chap. 10, 1:153–4.]

With Miss Temple gone in Mr. Nasmyth's post-chaise, Jane realizes that, for her, principles have meaning primarily within a human context, although they spring from divine order. She begins 'to feel the stirring of old emotions. It did not seem as if a prop were withdrawn, but rather as if a motive were gone: it was not the power to be tranquil which had failed me, but the reason for tranquillity was no more. My world had for some years been in Lowood; my experience had been of its rules and systems; now I remembered that the real world was wide, and that a varied field of hopes and fears, of sensations and excitements, awaited those who had courage to go forth into its expanse to seek real knowledge of life amidst its perils.' [Chap. 10, 1:154–5.]

As Gateshead had become a prison earlier, so Lowood now suddenly seems a place of detention. From both these places and from Thornfield and Moor House, Jane, in a recurrent pattern of behaviour, flies when she feels their cramping restraint, until at last she finds her home at Ferndean, where principles of morality and human affection live hand-in-hand. Jane longs to surmount the peaks on the horizon of Lowood: 'all within their boundary of rock and heath seemed prison-ground, exile limits. . . . I desired liberty; for liberty I gasped; for liberty I uttered a prayer; it seemed scattered on the wind then faintly blowing. I abandoned it, and framed a humbler supplication; for change, stimulus: that petition, too, seemed swept off into vague space; "Then," I cried, half desperate, "Grant me at least a new servitude!" '

[Chap. 10, 1:155–6.] The final word may serve to indicate the growth of Jane's humility in her stay at Lowood.

The atmosphere of Lowood has taught Jane the necessary restraint of passion, but it has denied her the equally necessary outlets for emotion. Thornfield provides them in amplitude.

The setting of the Thornfield section is different from the two preceding ones because it is made at once more personal and more symbolic. 'Great houses and fine grounds require the presence of the proprietor,' [Chap. 11, 1:185] says Mrs. Fairfax in the first mention of Rochester in the novel. Like a lifeless body, the house without its master has an air of decay: 'To pass its threshold was to return to stagnation.' [Chap. 12, 1:221.] Its reanimation is accomplished with Rochester's spirited presence: 'Thornfield Hall was a changed place: no longer silent as a church, it echoed every hour or two to a knock at the door or a clang of the bell; . . . a rill from the outer world was flowing through it; it had a master: for my part, I liked it better.' [Chap. 13, 1:226–7.]

On a naturalistic level, Jane thinks of the house as taking its being from the presence of Rochester, but Miss Brontë moves beyond this to make a symbolic identification of house and master. Like Jane, Rochester senses his own identity with the house and returns to it with affection. The terrors hidden behind its battlements lose their power as he sees the prospect of a new life to negate the past for himself and the house: 'I like Thornfield; its antiquity; its retirement; its old crow-trees and thorn-trees; its grey façade, and lines of dark windows reflecting that metal welkin: and yet how long have I abhorred the very thought of it; shunned it like a great plague-house!' [Chap. 15, 1:282.]

Perhaps few readers notice on first acquaintance with the novel that Miss Brontë suggests the physical likenesses between the appearance of the square-faced Rochester and the prospect of the house. Both are impressive to look at but of modest dimensions with little pretension to physical beauty, and are characterized by apparent solidity and more than a little grimness. The house 'was three stories high, of proportions not vast, though considerable; a gentleman's manor-house, not a nobleman's seat: battlements round the top gave it a picturesque look. Its grey front stood out well from the back ground of a rookery, whose cawing tenants were now on the wing: they flew over the lawn and grounds to alight in a great meadow, from which these were separated by a sunk fence, and where an array of mighty old thorn trees, strong, knotty, and broad as oaks, at once explained the etymology of the mansion's designation.' [Chap. 11, I:183–4.] When she first sees Rochester at Thornfield, Jane recognizes him by 'his broad and jetty eyebrows; his square forehead, made squarer by the horizontal sweep of his black hair. I recognized his decisive nose, more remarkable for character than beauty; his full nostrils, denoting, I thought, choler; his grim mouth, chin, and jaw—yes, all three were very grim, and no mistake. His shape, now divested of cloak, I perceived harmonized in squareness with his physiognomy: I suppose it was a good figure in the athletic sense of the term—broad chested and thin flanked; though neither tall nor graceful.' [Chap. 13, I:230–31.]

As Jane is being shown the house, she goes last to the low, dark third story with its outdated furnishings; 'if there were a ghost at Thornfield Hall, this would be its haunt.' [Chap. 11, I:198.] Like its master, the house has been turned backward in time, and 'these relics gave to the third story of Thornfield Hall the aspect of a home of the past: a shrine of memory'. [Chap. 11, I:197.]

On this initial trip through the house, Jane dimly senses much that she is to know later with horrid certainty. Her perceptions about Thornfield are constantly used as foreshadowings of what she is to discover of its master. Long before she has any reason to believe that Rochester's blunt forehead masks a secret, she realizes that the house hides a terrible inhabitant behind its grey front.

As Jane keeps her silent post when Richard Mason suffers his mysterious wounds at the hands of his sister, Jane asks herself, 'What crime was this, that lived incarnate in this sequestered mansion, and could neither be expelled nor subdued by the owner? What mystery, that broke out, now in fire and now in blood, at the deadest hours of night? What creature was it, that, masked in an ordinary woman's face and shape, uttered the voice, now of a mocking demon, and anon of a carrion-seeking bird of prey?' [Chap. 20, II:120.]

When Rochester interrupts his curious account of Adèle's mother to glare at the house, he explains his frown to Jane by saying that he has been 'arranging a point with my destiny. She stood there, by that beech-trunk—a hag like one of those who appeared to Macbeth on the heath of Forres. "You like Thornfield?" she said, lifting her finger; and then she wrote in the air a memento, which ran in lurid hieroglyphics all along the house-front, between the upper and lower row of windows. "Like it if you can!" "Like it if you dare!"' [Chap. 15, I:283.]

There are other suggestions of the likeness between Rochester and Thornfield, such as the prophetic dream Jane has of the ruined house the night before she expects to be married. When she finally discovers the secret of Thornfield, it is also to discover the reality about Rochester. However, the most important use of the likeness between master and house occurs when Jane returns to Thornfield at the end of the book, expecting to see Rochester. ' "My first view of it shall be in front," I determined, "where its bold battlements will strike the eye nobly at once, and where I can single out my master's very window: perhaps he will be standing at it—he rises early: perhaps he is now walking in the orchard, or on the pavement in front. Could I but see him!—but a moment!" ' [Chap. 36, III:252.] On her arrival she 'looked with timorous joy towards a stately house: I saw a blackened ruin. . . . The front was, as I had once seen it in a dream, but a shell-like wall, very high and very fragile looking, perforated

with paneless windows: no roof, no battlements, no chimneys
—all had crashed in.' [Chap. 36, III:254.] At the level of
simple foreshadowing, the house is an emblem of the blinded,
blackened, shattered Rochester that she is to find at Ferndean. More powerfully, it is a visual gathering together of
the whole complex group of threads that have run through
the Thornfield section of the novel, a graphical portrayal of
the self-destruction wrought by an unhallowed passion. With
this kind of symbolic writing, Charlotte Brontë has broadened
the melodramatic story into a statement on the nature of sin,
and the statement is possible only after experience of the long
chain of associations that she has established.

With the long, slow oscillation of a pendulum, the story
has moved from one extreme, Gateshead, with its atmosphere of anger, sensuality, selfishness, terror, and the other
passions, to its antithesis, Lowood, redolent of hypocrisy
and starvation, relieved by an unworldly piety that takes no
more account of the senses and emotions that Mr. Brocklehurst himself would sanction. In the Thornfield and Moor
House sections, the pendulum swings to and fro between
extremes again before coming to rest at dead centre in Ferndean. But the passion of Thornfield is the more alluring one
of physical desire, calling itself love, and the hypocrisy of
Mr. Brocklehurst is replaced at Moor House by another kind
of religiosity with the more attractive name of self-sacrifice;
the extremes of human choice become dangerous for the first
time. If affection and high aspiration both mask selfishness,
they are equally perilous. Falstaff and Hotspur, as Shakespeare knew, pose equal threats to Prince Hal.

Jane Eyre is often described as a Gothic or neo-Gothic
romance, when in actuality those aspects of the novel are
important primarily in the Thornfield section, the long central part of the book, and are absent in the other four sections.
It is true, however, that Bertha's attempt to burn Rochester
in his bed, her attack on her brother, her menacing laugh,
and her surreptitious visit to tear Jane's wedding veil all

combine to create an aura that hangs over the rest of the book, so that in retrospect one thinks of the whole novel as coloured by the Gothic atmosphere, including those sections before we have even heard of Bertha and that which occurs after she has flung herself from the flaming battlements. The reason is not far to seek. The danger of the unreality of vision that man suffers when he gives himself over to unrestrained passion is one of the themes in the book, and Bertha becomes the objectification of the results of uninhibited licence. As passion is part of the non-rational (or subrational) faculties of man, it is closely allied to those other potent means by which man deceives himself: superstition, a belief in fairy-tales, the illusion that man's morality is wholly relative and unrelated to universal codes of conduct, and a credence in the superficial appearances of beauty. All of them become as unreal as fairy-tales or the wanderings of ghosts through haunted mansions, all of them throw a veil of illusion over the clear sight that man should cultivate.

To establish the relationships between Gateshead and Thornfield with their parallel auras of the non-rational, Miss Brontë first introduces Jane to the house in the tour of inspection when the third story induces in her something of the same *frisson* that she has felt in the red room in the other great house of the novel. More importantly, Rochester's introduction into the plot is in terms of Jane's memories of nursery stories and 'other rubbish'. As the sound of Rochester's horse approaches her in the lane to Hay, she remembers 'certain of Bessie's tales, wherein figured a North-of-England spirit, called a "Gytrash"; which, in the form of horse, mule, or large dog, haunted solitary ways, and sometimes called upon belated travellers, as this horse was now coming upon me.'

Among the other creatures present in her mind are 'the mighty mastiffs' of *Gulliver's Travels* as she listens to the horse's hoofs. 'It was very near, but not yet in sight; when, in addition to the tramp, tramp, I heard a rush under the hedge, and close down by the hazel stems glided a great dog, whose black and white colour made him a distinct object against the trees. It was exactly one mask of Bessie's Gytrash,—a lion-like creature with long hair and a huge head: it passed me, however, quietly enough; not staying to look up, with strange pretercanine eyes, in my face, as I half expected it would. The horse followed, — a tall steed, and on its back a rider. The man, the human being, broke the spell at once.'[1] [Chap. 12, 1:212–13.]

In spite of memories of Bessie's stories, Jane now has a mature reaction to superstition, and her innate common sense discards it at the sight of Rochester. The incident might stand as a microcosm of the whole Thornfield section, with Jane attracted to illusion, then sturdily putting it from her. After Rochester leaves her, Jane goes to Hay and returns to the stile: 'I stopped a minute, looked round and listened; with an idea that a horse's hoofs might ring on the causeway again, and that a rider in a cloak, and a Gytrash-like Newfoundland dog, might be again apparent: I saw only the hedge and a pollard willow before me, rising up still and straight to meet the moonbeams; I heard only the faintest waft of wind, roaming fitful among the trees round Thornfield, a mile distant; and when I glanced down in the direction of the murmur, my eye, traversing the hall-front, caught a light kindling in a window: it reminded me that I was late, and I hurried on.' [Chap. 12, 1:221.] Reality is seldom far away for Jane.

Although Jane has undergone the experiences at Gateshead and Lowood that enable her to resist illusion, to discount superstition and the other vagaries of the unhealthy mind, Rochester has not yet been schooled by his own life. The reality of his love for Jane is never called into question, but his plan to marry her bigamously is only an extension of his enslavement by Bertha and his succession of mistresses.

---

[1] Rochester, too, thinks 'unaccountably of fairy tales' when he first sees her, and wonders whether she has bewitched his horse.

In a world where common sense and religious feeling unite to produce reality, his bigamous intent is as unnatural, as uncontrolled as Jane's childhood superstitions. As if to show the faultiness of his intentions, he constantly addresses her in terms that remind us of the 'rubbish' of Jane's childhood reading: 'imp', 'elf', 'sprite', 'fairy', and 'changeling', while she steadfastly calls him 'Sir' or 'Mr. Rochester'. When Jane rejoins him at Ferndean, after he has learned to face the reality of his own guilt, he seldom addresses her in the old terms, except to ask in the incredulity of his happiness, 'You are altogether a human being, Jane? You are sure of that?' [Chap. 37, III:280] and to call her a 'mocking changeling' [Chap. 37, III:283] in obvious delight at the inappropriateness of the words, since she has just been talking of those most mundane nourishments, ham and eggs.

The basic unreality of Thornfield, built over the abyss of the secret that Rochester refuses to face, is reflected in the glittering, shallow houseparty that he assembles there; the artificiality and selfishness of the conversation reveals the unreality of the emotions beneath it. It would be idle to pretend that the talk of the Ingrams is like anything ever heard on land or sea, but it is not totally ineffective within the context of the novel, for it both reflects the emptiness of Blanche and her family and suggests, as has been noted before, that Jane, in her dislike of the Ingrams, remembers the conversation as more stilted than it actually was. The stylized, almost burlesqued speech is a parallel on the verbal level of the play-acting to which Rochester and his guests resort in order to forget their tedium.[1] Probably the only time that there is any honest communication with any of the guests is when Rochester, in the guise of the old gipsy woman, tells

[1] The charade of 'Bridewell', with successive scenes of a wedding, the gift of jewels to Rebecca, and a prison are naturally taken by Blanche, and perhaps Jane, to have special reference in real life to the two actors, Rochester and Blanche, at least in the first two scenes. Curiously, however, it has more premonitory significance for Jane and Rochester, since he offers jewels, takes her to the altar, and would be at least liable to imprisonment if he were to succeed in a bigamous marriage.

some home truths to Blanche and the other young ladies of the party. It is only to Jane that he can reveal himself and speak directly without a disguise.

The subtle balance between the love of Rochester and Jane, and the alluring falsity of the projected marriage is most tellingly suggested in the proposal scene in the garden. It is sunset on Midsummer-eve, 'sweet-briar and southern-wood, jasmine, pink, and rose have long been yielding their evening sacrifice of incense', [Chap. 23, II:199] moths hum by in the evening air, and the song of a nightingale floats over the enclosed, paradisiacal garden. 'No nook in the grounds,' writes Miss Brontë lest we miss the parallel, 'more sheltered and more Eden-like.' [Chap. 23, II:198.] The confessions of love are as new to Jane as they were to Eve. But the original Eden fell to grief through passion, and so does the garden of Thornfield. At Rochester's invocation of God's sanction on the marriage, the moon clouds over, and Rochester's face fades into the night. 'And what ailed the chestnut tree? it writhed and groaned; while wind roared in the laurel walk, and came sweeping over us.' [Chap. 23, II:214.] It is like a gigantic heaving of nature at Rochester's blasphemy; in the morning Adèle comes running to tell Jane 'that the great horse-chestnut at the bottom of the orchard had been struck by lightning in the night, and half of it split away'. [Chap. 23, II:216.] Only in retrospect do we see the significance of the fact that the proposal takes place on Mid-summer-eve, the night of enchantment when fairies rule the world of men. The emotions have been real, but they exist in a fairy-tale world.

To deny superstition is only to discount the fantasies born of man's brain, not to deny supernatural manifestations, as Helen Burns knows. In one of the central passages of the novel, Jane speculates on the meaning of the workings of the spiritual that she finds around her: 'Presentiments are strange things! and so are sympathies; and so are signs: and the three combined make one mystery to which humanity has not yet found the key. I never laughed at presentiments in my life; because I have had strange ones of my own. Sympathies, I believe, exist: (for instance, between far-distant, long-absent, wholly estranged relatives; asserting, notwithstanding their alienation, the unity of the source to which each traces his origin) whose workings baffle mortal comprehension. And signs, for aught we know, may be but the sympathies of Nature with man.' [Chap. 21, ii:140.] Jane's dreams, the shattered chestnut tree, the mysterious cry from Rochester that Jane hears at Moor House: these are as mysterious but as real as the ordering of the universe, and they are totally different from superstition. 'Down superstition!' commands Jane when she hears Rochester's cry. 'This is not thy deception, nor thy witchcraft: it is the work of nature. She was roused, and did–no miracle–but her best.' [Chap. 35, iii:245.]

Jane Eyre is at bottom, as the above quotation suggests, largely a religious novel, concerned with the meaning of religion to man and its relevance to his behaviour. Jane discovers at Lowood that she can comprehend religion only when it has some relation to man, but at Thornfield she sees the opposite error, of man attempting to remake religion to his own convenience.

The line between conventionality based on mere social propriety, and customary behaviour based on divine ordinance is as thin and as difficult of discernment as the division between Rochester's illicit desire for Jane and his natural love and need of her. 'In time, I think you will learn to be natural with me, as I find it impossible to be conventional with you,' [Chap. 14, i:274] he tells her. Certainly, conventionality is not the quality one associates with their relationship, with its conversations of staggering frankness and disregard of propriety that so startle and perplex good Mrs. Fairfax. In and out of each other's bedrooms they wander with never a thought of convention. On the deeper question of whether morality is equally a mere convention to be re-made according

to the circumstances of one's life, Jane and Rochester part
company.

Jane's moral steadfastness is early apparent to Rochester.
'I see genuine contentment in your gait and mien, your eye
and face, when you are helping me and pleasing me–working
for me, and with me, in, as you characteristically say, *"all
that is right"*: for if I bid you do what you thought wrong,
there would be no light-footed running, no neat-handed
alacrity, no lively glance and animated complexion. My
friend would turn to me, quiet and pale, and would say, "No,
sir; that is impossible: I cannot do it, because it is wrong;"
and would become immutable as a fixed star.' [Chap. 20,
II:133.]

Rochester's dilemma, however, is not the choice between
simple right and wrong, and he puts a case to Jane, thinking
of his disastrous first marriage: 'The results of what you
have done become in time to you utterly insupportable; you
take measures to obtain relief: unusual measures, but neither
unlawful nor culpable . . . you make a new acquaintance
. . . Such society revives, regenerates: you feel better days
come back–higher wishes, purer feelings; you desire to recommence your life, and to spend what remains to you of
days in a way more worthy of an immortal being. To attain
this end, are you justified in overleaping an obstacle of custom–a mere conventional impediment, which neither your
conscience sanctifies nor your judgment approves?' Jane's
response is like an echo of the counsel of Helen Burns: ' "Sir,"
I answered, "a Wanderer's repose or a Sinner's reformation
should never depend on a fellow-creature. Men and women
die; philosophers falter in wisdom, and Christians in goodness: if any one you know has suffered and erred, let him look
higher than his equals for strength to amend, and solace to
heal." ' [Chap. 20, II:135-7.] The question, of course, is the
old one of whether an immoral action is justified by a moral
objective, and Jane's answer is the traditional one, based upon
her own experience at Gateshead and Lowood, where she had

tried to make her own law by fighting tyranny with anger. The aftermath, as she knows, can only be bitter.

Those critics who have suggested that Miss Brontë has dodged the real issue of the novel by having Jane leave Rochester until his first wife is dead have neglected the careful structure of the plot up to this point. The issue is never whether Jane should become Rochester's mistress. To settle for nothing less than the best is not to be narrow; the test is to become worthy of love, not to take it on any terms but to deserve it: not to violate one's own nature and morality but so to expand that nature that it deserves reward. Jane and Rochester, learning to respect the inviolability of the soul as much as earthly delights, become a microcosm of man's striving for Christian reward.

This is not to suggest that Jane's problem is an easier one than Rochester's, even if her knowledge of the proper solution is always with her in the midst of temptation. 'My future husband was becoming to me my whole world; and more than the world: almost my hope of heaven,' she tells us during her engagement. 'He stood between me and every thought of religion, as an eclipse intervenes between man and the broad sun. I could not, in those days, see God for his creature of whom I had made an idol.' [Chap. 24, ii:252.] The divine injunction against idolatry returns to her mind when she realizes that she must leave Rochester. 'Terrible moment: full of struggle, blackness, burning! Not a human being that ever lived could wish to be loved better than I was loved; and him who thus loved me I absolutely worshipped: and I must renounce love and idol.' [Chap. 27, iii:36–7.]

Jane's final position on relative morality is given in her long, indomitable reply to her nagging realization that she is alone in the world and can injure no one else if she lives with Rochester: 'The more solitary, the more friendless, the more unsustained I am, the more I will respect myself. I will keep the law given by God; sanctioned by man. I will hold to the principles received by me when I was sane, and not mad—as

I am now. Laws and principles are not for the times when there is no temptation: they are for such moments as this, when body and soul rise in mutiny against their rigour: stringent are they; inviolate they shall be. If at my individual convenience I might break them, what would be their worth? They have a worth—so I have always believed; and if I cannot believe it now, it is because I am insane—quite insane: with my veins running fire, and my heart beating faster than I can count its throbs. Preconceived opinions, foregone determinations, are all that I have at this hour to stand by: there I plant my foot.' [Chap, 27, III:39–40.] Her morality is not a cowardly bowing down to convention but an heroic assertion of the sanctity of the individual soul. Jane's problem, then, becomes the precise opposite of Rochester's, for she must decide to injure him in cleaving to her own moral principles.

Jane's lonely and terrible wandering before she comes to Moor House is the most vivid of the *entr'actes* of the book, and it takes much of its colouring from its likeness to Lear's suffering on the heath; in each case the protagonist leaves a home that he has been assured would be his throughout life, turns to a nature that seems at first to be friendlier than man, then suffers its pitiless buffeting, and is at last taken in to be sheltered by compassionate fellow men on whom he has no claim. Both are convinced that their actions are right, both gnawed by the fear of having injured those who have wronged them. The likeness between the two is presumably not accidental, since Shakespeare's tragic king was clearly much in Miss Brontë's mind when she was writing the book. Her inveterate habit of quoting tags from her favourite authors—occasionally irrelevantly—is useful in establishing her current interest in *Lear*. Rochester echoes Lear as he removes his gipsy disguise: 'Off, ye lendings!' [Chap. 19, II:103] and Jane twice paraphrases Cordelia's lament over her father's ill-treatment:

> *Was this a face*
> *To be opposed against the warring winds?*
> *To stand against the deep dread-bolted thunder?*
>   . . .   *Mine enemy's dog,*
> *Though he had bit me, should have stood that night*
> *Against my fire.*

When she is taken in by the Rivers family, Jane says to Diana, 'If I were a masterless and stray dog, I know that you would not turn me from your hearth to-night: as it is, I really have no fear,' [Chap. 28, III:76] and she reproaches Hannah by accusing her of turning her away from the door, 'on a night when you should not have shut out a dog'. [Chap. 29, III:85.] On her first night on the moor, Jane says that 'Nature seemed to me benign and good: I thought she loved me, outcast as I was; and I, who from man could anticipate only mistrust, rejection, insult, clung to her with filial fondness.' [Chap. 28, III:51.] The parallels with Lear are useful to Miss Brontë both in establishing Jane's cosmic loneliness, adrift with not even a Fool to comfort her, and in heightening her horror, like that of Lear, of being unjust to the one person who loves her most. 'Gentle reader, may you never feel what I then felt! May your eyes never shed such stormy, scalding, heart-wrung tears as poured from mine. May you never appeal to Heaven in prayers so hopeless and so agonized as in that hour left my lips: for never may you, like me, dread to be the instrument of evil to what you wholly love.' [Chap. 27, III:48.]

As Rochester has been the ultimate temptation to Jane to live by passion alone, so St. John Rivers is to provide the final temptation to renounce the flesh entirely. His is a far subtler version of the spirit of Lowood and Mr. Brocklehurst because he is no hypocrite. Brocklehurst advocates mortification of the flesh for others while sacrificing nothing for himself and his family; St. John is harder on himself than on any one else. When it does not come into conflict with his own ambitious spirituality, he is capable of great kindness, and it is he who rescues Jane from death by exposure. Most of all, he is an integral part of the family that takes in Jane, first to a figurative membership in the first admirable family she has known, and then into a literal membership in the circle. The attraction of the Rivers family is doubled by its contrast to the only families she has previously known. At Gateshead she was among the Reeds, divided against each other, unloving and unlovable. At Lowood she has seen the Misses Brocklehurst, whose ostrich plumes and curled hair conceal heads of singular emptiness. At Thornfield she is the object of the scorn of the selfish Ingrams. The Rivers family is bound closely by love, they have unostentatious pride in themselves, they are handsome, and even somewhat scholarly.[1] There is an innate sympathy between Jane and her cousins that she feels instinctively is too strong to be accident. On discovering their relationship, she sees the moving power behind her wanderings as the sympathy 'between far-distant, long-absent, wholly estranged relatives; asserting, notwithstanding their alienation, the unity of the source to which each traces his origin.' 'Circumstances knit themselves, fitted themselves, shot into order: the chain that had been lying hitherto a formless lump of links, was drawn out straight,—every ring was perfect, the connection complete.' [Chap. 33, III:170.] Since Providence has brought them together, it is difficult for Jane to be sure that it has not also intended her as the wife of St. John. Only when St. John invokes God's name in support of a false ideal of marriage, as Rochester has done in the garden scene at Thornfield, does the supernatural intervene. This time, instead of manifesting itself through the destruction of the chestnut tree, Providence speaks through the mys-

[1] Probably Miss Brontë intends a distinction between the sisters, who retain their enthusiasm and their love of German poetry while learning the language in order to further their careers, and St. John, who learns Hindostanee by rote for use in his missionary work, with no apparent interest in it beyond its utility. Certainly, there is a vast contrast between Diana's ability as a teacher and that of St. John. Jane loves sitting at Diana's feet learning German, but she considers her tuition in Hindostanee an unloved servitude.

terious voice of Rochester carried on the wind. The chapter ends with Jane's falling on her knees in prayer, 'a different way to St. John's, but effective in its own fashion'. [Chap. 35, III:245.]

Mrs. Tillotson has pointed out that Miss Brontë quietly links the overt arrogance of Brocklehurst and the concealed egoism of St. John by using the same figure to describe them, that of the tall column or pillar.[1] Mr. Brocklehurst looks like black marble, but St. John, with his Greek face, classic nose, and Athenian mouth and chin, has a forehead of 'white stone'. 'I saw he was of the material from which nature hews her heroes—Christian and Pagan—her lawgivers, her statesmen, her conquerors: a steadfast bulwark for great interests to rest upon; but, at the fireside, too often a cold cumbrous column, gloomy and out of place.' [Chap. 34, III:188.] When he lies watchfully on the grass waiting for Jane to accept his bloodless offer of marriage, she sees him 'still as a prostrate column'. [Chap. 34, III:214.]

One is reminded of the story told of a famous twentieth-century Archbishop of Canterbury who ran headlong into the obdurate resistance to change of one of the older and more conservative bishops of his Church; after days of failing to change the Bishop's mind, the Archbishop finally remarked: 'The Bishop of —— inevitably reminds me of that great Christian, St. Simeon Stylites, for he has all the asceticism of the saint and all the rigidity of the pillar.' The remark summarizes Miss Brontë's attitude to Rivers.[2]

The unnatural quality of Brocklehurst is indicated by his attitude to 'naturally' curly hair; the equivalent aspect of St. John is his lack of response to the natural world. 'I think,

[1] P. 310. Swinburne also noticed that both men are described as being hewn of stone ('A Note on Charlotte Brontë', *Complete Works*, Bonchurch Edition, ed. Edmund Gosse and T. J. Wise, XIV, 31, William Heinemann Ltd., London; Gabriel Wells, New York, 1926.)

[2] The association of haughtiness with the stiffness of a pillar is repeated in the description of Lady Ingram in Chapter 17, where she is said to have a Roman countenance, with a double chin that disappears into 'a throat like a pillar'. Her arrogance is, of course, social not religious.

moreover, that Nature was not to him that treasury of delight it was to his sisters. He expressed once, and but once in my hearing, a strong sense of the rugged charm of the hills, and an inborn affection for the dark roof and hoary walls he called his home: but there was more of gloom than pleasure in the tone and words in which the sentiment was manifested; and never did he seem to roam the moors for the sake of their soothing silence—never seek out or dwell upon the thousand peaceful delights they could yield.' [Chap. 30, III:104.]

We are reminded of Lowood by the sense of cold that surrounds St. John, who says of himself that he is 'hard and cold'. [Chap. 34, III:188.] Repeatedly, his manners are described as 'chilling', 'freezing', 'icy', and his displeasure is the breaking up of a 'frozen sea'. He continually divorces himself from the fireside at Moor House, where he is a cold, out-of-place presence, to plunge into the winter weather on his parish rounds. He has none of the warmth of spirit of his sisters, and he deliberately cuts himself off from Rosamond Oliver, the only person for whom he feels a flicker of warm affection. 'Know me to be what I am,' he tells Jane, 'a cold, hard man.' [Chap. 32, III:152.]

Rochester has offered Jane love without marriage, St. John offers her marriage without love. The two men are hardly mirror images, however, for Rochester is capable of reformation, since he can sympathize with Jane's need for the part of the relationship that he cannot offer her; for natures unlike his own, St. John has nothing but contempt. Jane wishes to please Rivers, for she feels real admiration for him, 'but to do so, I felt daily more and more that I must disown half my nature', [Chap. 34, III:200] the half of her that cries out for feeling and human love.

In presenting this forbidding but compelling picture of a nature warped by a narrow and bigoted religiosity, Miss Brontë stresses St. John's intelligence, his disinterested charity, even his extreme good looks, nullified though they are by the marble heart within. The admiration that Jane feels for half his nature does not seem forced. But to complete the picture, he is compared to Brocklehurst and to that other figure of warped piety, Eliza Reed, who leaves England, as St. John does, in her case to become a Roman Catholic nun. Both Eliza and St. John despise hypocrisy and are quite open in their sacrifice of others to their own spiritual ambition. Eliza casts off Georgiana, just as St. John casts off his own family. Both of them live by precise rote, carrying out their religious duties without deriving from them any broadening of their natures. In matters of religion Eliza is a 'rigid formalist: no weather ever prevented the punctual discharge of what she considered her devotional duties; fair or foul, she went to church thrice every Sunday, and as often on weekdays as there were prayers'. [Chap. 21, II:175.] We are clearly meant to be reminded of Eliza when Jane says of St. John that 'he was comparatively seldom at home: a large proportion of his time appeared devoted to visiting the sick and poor among the scattered population of his parish. No weather seemed to hinder him in these pastoral excursions: rain or fair, he would, when his hours of morning study were over, take his hat, and, followed by his father's old pointer, Carlo, go out on his mission of love or duty—I scarcely know in which light he regarded it. . . . Zealous in his ministerial labours, blameless in his life and habits, he yet did not appear to enjoy that mental serenity, that inward content, which should be the reward of every sincere Christian and practical philanthropist.' [Chap. 30, III:103–4.]

When Jane returns to Gateshead and finds her two female cousins grown into repulsive, selfish women, she knows the reason for their natures: 'True, generous feeling is made small account of by some: but here were two natures rendered, the one intolerably acrid, the other despicably savourless for the want of it. Feeling without judgment is a washy draught indeed; but judgment untempered by feeling is too bitter and husky a morsel for human deglutition.' [Chap. 21,

II:174.] The condemnation of the two sisters colours one's feelings about St. John, who says arrogantly: 'Reason, and not Feeling, is my guide.'[1] [Chap. 32, III:152.]

The narrowness of St. John's religion keeps it from giving him any consolation, and it also prevents him from helping others. When Jane first hears him preach, she is impressed by his zeal and his power of language in the pulpit, but they bring no balm to the heart. 'Throughout there was a strange bitterness; an absence of consolatory gentleness: stern allusions to Calvinistic doctrines—election, predestination, reprobation—were frequent; and each reference to these points sounded like a sentence pronounced for doom. When he had done, instead of feeling better, calmer, more enlightened by his discourse, I experienced an inexpressible sadness.' [Chap. 30, III:105.]

Eliza and St. John presumably both love God (perhaps even with the whole of their cramped hearts), but they scarcely love their neighbours as themselves. Eliza is small-souled, St. John large-souled, but they are alike in their neglect of human affections. Romanism and Calvinism, Miss Brontë's twin abominations, are here exposed as being equally selfish. For both of them, what goes by the name of self-sacrifice ultimately means the sacrifice of others.

The mood of the closing section at Ferndean is of reconciliation, and, like all such scenes, this one has overtones of temporizing, of lessons learned, that give it a quiet, autumnal quality. It is hard to remember that the Jane of this section is still only nineteen years old, perhaps because her attitudes have matured and become those of the older Jane who is the real narrator of the novel. There is little of the youthful, lyric quality of the proposal scene in the garden at Thornfield, for both Jane and Rochester have learned to face life

[1] There is probably a further parallel between St. John and Eliza in his repudiation of the physical beauty of Rosamond, and in Eliza's disgust at Georgiana's interest in her own appearance. Eliza is restrained to the point of asceticism in her own dress, in a way that would presumably appease even Mr. Brocklehurst.

directly without illusion and to make happiness out of a human lot that is less than lyric. To Rochester's question, 'You are altogether a human being, Jane?' she answers, 'I conscientiously believe so, Mr. Rochester.'

Miss Brontë never wrote a more sure and successful scene than this reunion of lovers battered by life. One shudders to think of the sea of pathos in which some Victorian novelists, even writers like Dickens or Trollope, might have drowned the reunion. Rochester is maimed and blinded, a pitiful creature who must be led wherever he goes, but the reader is never invited either to sentimentalize over him or to disregard the brute facts of his humiliation. In part Miss Brontë achieves her effect by turning the tables on Rochester and investing Jane with the same teasing tone that he has taken with her earlier.

Brusqueness, teasing, and plain speaking throughout the novel have always been the mark of sincerity. Even before she knows who he is, Jane says of the horseman in the lane to Hay: 'the frown, the roughness of the traveller set me at my ease', [Chap. 12, 1:216] and a few pages later when she is introduced to Rochester at Thornfield, she reflects of his gruff greeting: 'I sat down quite disembarrassed. A reception of finished politeness would probably have confused me.' [Chap. 13, 1:231.] She is never misled into mistaking his brusquerie for brutality. He asks her, 'And will you consent to dispense with a great many conventional forms and phrases, without thinking that the omission arises from insolence?' Responding both from her immediate knowledge of what sort of man he is, and from her own innate feeling of equality, she reassures him: 'I am sure, sir, I should never mistake informality for insolence: one I rather like, the other nothing free-born would submit to, even for a salary.' [Chap. 14, 1:264.] Even when he first proposes to her, Rochester speaks the blunt truth (too blunt for many modern readers, used to more insincerity in fiction): 'You—poor and obscure, and small and plain as you are—I entreat to accept me as a husband.'

Astonished as she is, Jane begins 'in his earnestness – and especially in his incivility – to credit his sincerity'.[1] [Chap. 23, ii:212.]

When he can no longer swagger, Rochester find his role and Jane's reversed. In anguish he asks her: 'Am I hideous, Jane?' The answer is prompt: 'Very, sir: you always were, you know.' [Chap. 37, iii:282.] Her tone, like that of Rochester earlier in the novel, covers a sentiment too deep for tears or protestation. Clear-sighted as she is, Jane knows exactly what she is doing, and her charming teasing of him about St. John Rivers is undertaken deliberately. 'Jealousy had got hold of him: she stung him; but the sting was salutary: it gave him respite from the gnawing fang of melancholy. I would not, therefore, immediately charm the snake.' [Chap. 37, iii:289.] Just as his brusqueness has reassured her earlier, now her impishness tells him more of her love than endearments could do.

In the greatest of novels, particularly novels of development, the revelation of character comes as an unfolding of the inevitable, not as an arbitrary wrench by the author. There is constant surprised pleasure in re-reading *Jane Eyre* to see how carefully Miss Brontë has given early indications of later character development, as well as foreshadowings of the plot. The bluntness with which Jane has answered Mrs. Reed and Brocklehurst has flowered into the marvellously independent speech of a woman who can, in her self-assurance, be so spon-

---

[1] Incivil he perhaps is and certainly tactless, but not for the reasons that most readers seem to think. His impoliteness actually lies in paraphrasing Jane's own words of a short time before, when she describes herself as 'poor, obscure, plain, and little' (for the rest of the quotation, see p. 93). It seems reasonable to assume that the words are meant to be spoken in a tender manner, even though Jane does not accept the tenderness or has forgotten her own words, as most readers have. Whatever else Rochester is guilty of at this juncture, he is not falling into bathos in his speech, as Lord David Cecil thinks (*Early Victorian Novelists*, p. 121).

A similar repetition of words spoken in deep emotion occurs near the end of *Villette*, in Chapter 41, after Lucy has complained of not seeing Paul 'all these weary days'. Three times Paul repeats her phrase 'with a gentle, kindly mimicry' of her 'voice and foreign accent . . . of which the playful banter never wounded'.

taneously and devilishly gay with her future husband. The
quality of their love-making at Ferndean is the fruition of
Jane's mental resolve at Thornfield about her behaviour
during her engagement: 'I like you more than I can say; but
I'll not sink into a bathos of sentiment: and with this needle
of repartee I'll keep you from the edge of the gulph too.'
[Chap. 24, II:250.] Her earlier manner is dictated by caution,
now it grows naturally out of assurance, but in both cases
the quality is the same. Miss Brontë's language is as reso-
lutely anti-sentimental as her themes.

Jane's assurance springs, of course, out of love, a love between emotional and spiritual equals. The novel is frequently
cited as the earliest major feminist novel, although there is
not a hint in the book of any desire for political, legal, educa-
tional, or even intellectual equality between the sexes. Miss
Brontë asks only for the simple – or is it the most complex? –
recognition that the same heart and the same spirit animate
both men and women, and that love is the pairing of equals
in these spheres. 'I don't think, sir,' she tells Rochester early
in their association, 'you have a right to command me,
merely because you are older than I, or because you have
seen more of the world than I have – your claim to superiority
depends on the use you have made of your time and experience.' [Chap. 14, I:262–3.] When she thinks that he is
about to marry Blanche, she bursts out at him: 'Do you think,
because I am poor, obscure, plain, and little, I am soulless
and heartless? – You think wrong! – I have as much soul as
you, – and full as much heart! . . . I am not talking to you
now through the medium of custom, conventionalities, nor
even of mortal flesh: – it is my spirit that addresses your
spirit; just as if both had passed through the grave, and we
stood at God's feet, equal, – as we are!' [Chap. 23, II:209.]
The famous plea that women ought not to be confined 'to
making pudding and knitting stockings, to playing on the
piano and embroidering bags' [Chap. 12, I:207] is not
propaganda for equal employment but for a recognition of

woman's emotional nature. The condemnation of women to a place apart results in the creation of empty, capricious women like Blanche Ingram, who tyrannize over men whenever possible, indulge in dreams of Corsair lovers, and can communicate only in the Byronic language of outdated romantic fiction. Only equals like Jane and Rochester dare to speak truth couched in language of unadorned directness.

If the development of Jane's character to mature womanhood is as inevitable as it is direct, so is that of Rochester, who grows to true manliness, though divested of the romantic trappings of virility. For all Jane's temptations, she is enabled to resist the worst of them through the conscience developed during her early experiences, and because she relies upon what she knows of divine law. Rochester's development, however, is from sin to repentance, passing from flagrant transgressions of the moral law, through the stage of a morality of expediency when he attempts to bend divine law to sanctify his own wishes, to the humility of repentance.

'Mr. Rochester has a thoughtful nature and a very feeling heart,' wrote his creator to W. S. Williams; 'he is neither selfish nor self-indulgent; he is ill-educated, misguided; errs, when he does err, through rashness and inexperience: he lives for a time as too many other men live, but being radically better than most men, he does not like that degraded life, and is never happy in it. He is taught the severe lessons of experience and has sense to learn wisdom from them. Years improve him; the effervescence of youth foamed away, what is really good in him still remains. His nature is like wine of a good vintage, time cannot sour, but only mellows him. Such at least was the character I meant to portray.' [Shorter, 1:446.]

The modern temptation in reading this novel is to forgive Rochester for his life of dissipation on the grounds that the failure of his first marriage is not his fault. Clearly, this was not the view of Miss Brontë, for she goes to considerable trouble to indicate that he marries in accordance with the conventions of society, and 'the prurience, the rashness, the

blindness of youth.' The marriage to Bertha is arranged for
financial gain, and Rochester, who 'seldom saw her alone,
and had very little private conversation with her', is carried
away by the pride of conquest and passion. 'I was dazzled,
stimulated: my senses were excited; and being ignorant, raw,
and inexperienced, I thought I loved her.' [Chap. 27, III:17.]
In taking his three mistresses (who are perhaps to be excused,
since none of them had the advantages of English upbringing
and education), he lowers himself to the level of his inferiors, 'for I began to regard the notion of an intellectual,
faithful, loving woman as a mere dream'. [Chap. 27, III:30.]

In the second stage of his growth, when he meets Jane, he
first feels the sting of remorse, 'the poison of life'. When Jane
suggests that repentance is the cure for remorse, he answers:
'It is not its cure. Reformation may be its cure; and I could
reform—I have strength yet for that—if—but where is the use
of thinking of it, hampered, burdened, cursed as I am? Besides, since happiness is irrevocably denied me, I have a right
to get pleasure out of life: and I *will* get it, cost what it may.'
[Chap. 14, I:268.]

The third stage is, of course, reached after his terrible
suffering in seeing Jane leave him, and then in the loss of his
sight and strength, a loss both physically maiming and
spiritually healing. 'Divine justice pursued its course,' he
recollects in humility; 'disasters came thick on me: I was
forced to pass through the valley of the shadow of death. *His*
chastisements are mighty; and one smote me which has
humbled me for ever.' [Chap. 37, III:298.] The holocaust of
Thornfield becomes a ritualistic purging of his sin in which,
through his suffering, he is relieved of Bertha, the burden of
his past, leaving him, like the house, as Jane had seen it in
her dream, 'but a shell-like wall, very high and very fragile
looking, perforated with paneless windows: no roof, no
battlements, no chimneys—all had crashed in.' [Chap. 36,
III:254.] In novelistic technique the house has fused with
Rochester in a symbol of harsh penance; in the sensibility of

Jane, its burning becomes one of the signs demonstrating 'the sympathies of Nature with man', in company with the blasted chestnut tree and Rochester's echoing midnight cry.

'I am no better than the old lightning-struck chestnut-tree in Thornfield orchard,' Rochester says in his crippled condition. 'And what right would that ruin have to bid a budding woodbine cover its decay with freshness?' Jane, who has seen the great tree 'black and riven: the trunk, split down the centre', rising from the 'adhesion at the faithful, honest roots', [Chap. 25, II:256–7] senses his spiritual health: 'You are no ruin, sir–no lightning-struck tree: you are green and vigorous. Plants will grow about your roots, whether you ask them or not, because they take delight in your bountiful shadow; and as they grow they will lean towards you, and wind round you, because your strength offers them so safe a prop.' [Chap. 37, III:294–5.] The significance of the chestnut tree is strengthened and made more credible because it has been recognized separately by both a bluff middle-aged man and a young girl.

It is, however, the mysterious summons borne on the wind that prompts Rochester to his most explicit statement of his changed views: 'When you rose upon me so unexpectedly last night, I had difficulty in believing you any other than a mere voice and vision: something that would melt to silence and annihilation, as the midnight whisper and mountain echo had melted before. Now I thank God! I know it to be otherwise. Yes, I thank God!' [Chap. 37, III:301–2.] Gross superstition has been replaced by a belief in the supernatural, 'an invisible world and a kingdom of spirits'.

Falling on his knees, he asks strength to lead a new life henceforth, and then 'he stretched his hand out to be led. I took that dear hand, held it a moment to my lips, then let it pass round my shoulder: being so much lower of stature than he, I served both for his prop and guide. We entered the wood, and wended homeward.' [Chap. 37, III:302.] Like an echo of the end of *Paradise Lost* they enter a new life, putting behind them the illicit Eden of the garden at Thornfield, all forbidden passion spent.

Illicit passion is over but not lawful married love. Miss Brontë's adored Thackeray once lamented the impossibility in his own time of writing frankly of a young man's sexual appetites; he could hardly entertain the idea of suggesting their existence in decent women. For an ear attuned to the accents of dignified acquiescence in the voices of early Victorian heroines as they accept marriage, it is startling to hear Jane's open celebration of complete love in notes as natural and spontaneous as those of Juliet awaiting her wedding night. No wonder that some of Miss Brontë's contemporaries found her coarse. Even more telling than Jane's rhapsodic accounts of her own love are the countless times that she and Rochester reach out to touch each other as if to reassure themselves of the other's physical presence. When they meet at Ferndean, the conversation is counterpointed by a series of explorations of each other's bodies, as Rochester's tentative hands recognize successively her fingers, arm, shoulder, neck, waist, limbs, and features ('This is her shape—this is her size—'). Jane sits running her fingers through his uncut hair, looking at his mutilated arm, touching his singed eyebrows, and, of course, kissing him as she refuses to leave the knee on which she is sitting. When he asks Jane if he suits her, she answers: 'To the finest fibre of my nature, sir,' and Rochester, whose 'old impetuosity was rising,' says at once: 'We must become one flesh without delay, Jane: there is but the licence to get—then we marry.' [Chap. 37, iii:297.] In the coda to the novel, Jane says with all the happiness of a well-wed woman: 'I have now been married ten years. I know what it is to live entirely for and with what I love best on earth. I hold myself supremely blest—blest beyond what language can express; because I am my husband's life as fully as he is mine. No woman was ever nearer to her mate than I am: ever more absolutely bone of his bone, and flesh of his flesh.' [Chap. 38, iii:307.] There have been more detailed accounts of physical love since Miss Brontë wrote those lines, but few more frank. The harmony of body and spirit is complete.

The Miltonic resonance of the lovers' walk back to Ferndean may serve to remind us of the last of the major literary invocations that Miss Brontë makes in the novel, that of Samson. Shortly after Jane and Rochester have pledged their love at Thornfield, Jane, in teasing reference to the history of his mistresses and to her own influence over him, says to Rochester, 'I was thinking of Hercules and Samson with their charmers –' [Chap. 24, ii:225.] When she refuses to live with him after the discovery of Bertha's existence, Rochester finds the 'knot' in Jane's character: 'By God! I long to exert a fraction of Samson's strength, and break the entanglement like tow!' [Chap. 27, iii:11.] The allusions to the Hebrew hero are without much significance at the time, and, indeed, it is only in retrospect that it appears. However, Miss Brontë has already begun establishing the connection that she is to use later.

When Jane stands looking for the first time at Ferndean Manor, the door opens and the blinded Rochester comes forth, his 'athletic strength' apparently still unquelled. 'But in his countenance, I saw a change: that looked desperate and brooding – that reminded me of some wronged and fettered wild-beast or bird, dangerous to approach in his sullen woe. The caged eagle, whose gold-ringed eyes cruelty has extinguished, might look as looked that sightless Samson.' [Chap. 37, iii:268.] Rochester must now be led forth, like the hero at the beginning of Milton's drama, and he grieves to Jane: 'You know I was proud of my strength: but what is it now, when I must give it over to foreign guidance, as a child does its weakness?' [Chap. 37, iii:298.] When he is hoping desperately that Jane still loves him, he murmurs: 'My seared vision! My crippled strength!' [Chap. 37, iii:294.] Like the Biblical hero, still more like the Miltonic Samson, he has been the creature of physical passion and he has sinned in attempting to substitute his own will for that of

God. Rochester might say with the blinded Gloucester, in words equally applicable to Samson: 'I stumbled when I saw.'

Rochester and Milton's Samson are both essentially New Testament heroes, suffering that they may at last come to the service of God, crushed as His servants not as vengeful supermen. Both writers take liberties with the legend for their own purposes. There is a hint of the messenger's account of Samson's death in the report by the old butler of the collapse of Thornfield and the maiming of its titular master, who has been slave to its hidden inhabitant: 'As he came down the great stair-case at last, after Mrs. Rochester had flung herself from the battlements, there was a great crash—all fell. He was taken out from under the ruins, alive, but sadly hurt: a beam had fallen in such a way as to protect him partly; but one eye was knocked out, and one hand so crushed that Mr. Carter, the surgeon, had to amputate it directly. The other eye inflamed: he lost the sight of that also. He is now helpless, indeed—blind and a cripple.' [Chap. 36, III:263–4.]

For, of course, Rochester is not killed in the crash of his temple around him, although his sinful and selfish nature perishes there. The whole use of the Samson story in the novel serves as evocative suggestion, not as strict parallel, and cannot be pressed too far on a level of literal correspondence. What it does, rather, is to give dignity and significance to the account of an individual who is part of the great archetypal pattern of sin, suffering, and redemption. With this in mind, one has difficulty in finding patience for accounts of the novel that try to see it in terms of twentieth-century psychology, finding in it feminine-masculine antagonisms, with Jane finally triumphing by reducing Rochester to helplessness, so that she can assume the role of dominant mother-figure.[1] It does not seem to me too revolutionary to feel that

[1] For one such account, see Martin S. Day, 'Central Concepts of *Jane Eyre*', *Personalist*, Autumn 1960, vol. XLI, no. 4, pp. 495–505. He feels that the maiming of Rochester 'suggests symbolic emasculation, as it most certainly reduces the dominant male to the dependent child'.

sin, suffering, and redemption may loom larger than sexual rivalry in Christian thought.

Rochester emerges at the end of the novel as considerably more than the mere lover of the central character; he is her complement, filling out her vision of the world. On a lesser scale, the other characters of the book fulfil the same novelistic function.

Of those characters not yet discussed in some detail, the most interesting is that irritating young woman Blanche Ingram, with her satirical laugh, her condescension to Jane and snubbing of the footman, and her habit—surely unparalleled in fiction, let alone life—of calling her mother 'Baroness Ingram, of Ingram Park'. Blanche is of the group of women, like Caroline in *The Professor*, who are described as exotic, Oriental temptresses. With telegraphic brevity, Mrs. Fairfax sketches her for Jane: 'Tall, fine bust, sloping shoulders; long, graceful neck; olive complexion, dark and clear; noble features; eyes rather like Mr. Rochester's: large and black, and as brilliant as her jewels. And then she had such a fine head of hair; raven-black.' [Chap. 16, II:14.] In the painting that Jane makes from this description, she does not fail to include 'the raven ringlets, the oriental eye'. [Chap. 16, II:18.] The essential Blanche is revealed in her character as Rebecca in the charade, when she is 'attired in oriental fashion: a crimson scarf tied sash-like round the waist; an embroidered handkerchief knotted about her temples; her beautifully-moulded arms bare, one of them up-raised in the act of supporting a pitcher, poised gracefully on her head. Both her cast of form and feature, her complexion and her general air, suggested the idea of some Israelitish princess of the patriarchal days.' [Chap. 18, II:64.] She feeds on romantic fiction ('Know that I doat on Corsairs') and her vision of marriage is one of pure adulation: 'I am resolved my husband shall not be a rival, but a foil to me. I will suffer no competitor near the throne; I shall exact an undivided homage: his devotions shall not be shared between me and the shape he sees in

his mirror.' [Chap. 17, ɪɪ:56.] In short, she is the socially
acceptable version of Rochester's wife and his un-English
mistresses, and, like them, her motive in flirting with him is
financial gain.

Unfortunately for her, Miss Ingram, in acting her part as
romantic heroine, overacts. Jane is grimly amused at her
'efforts at fascinating Mr. Rochester; to witness their repeated failure–herself unconscious that they did fail; vainly
fancying that each shaft launched, hit the mark, and infatua-
tedly pluming herself on success, when her pride and self-
complacency repelled further and further what she wished to
allure'. [Chap. 18, ɪɪ:70–71.] Rochester's own objective
view of the lady's physical charms is contained in his description of her as a 'strapper–a real strapper, Jane: big, brown,
and buxom; with hair just such as the ladies of Carthage must
have had'. [Chap. 20, ɪɪ:138.] On another occasion he calls
her 'an extensive armful'. [Chap. 23, ɪɪ:203.] Rochester's
treatment of Blanche is one of the least attractive aspects of
his character, for he deliberately encourages her when he
feels nothing in return. Emotionally he is indefensible, but
thematically it may be said that he is treating her exactly as
he does Céline, Giacinta, and Clara: he has yet to realize
fully that women can be his equals, and he treats them as
inferior beings whose interest in him is financial and who
interest him only sensually.

Blanche stands, too, for Jane as an example of what happens to women whose selfish interest is chiefly monetary and
physical. When Rochester is buying her the inappropriate
finery for her wedding journey, he says in delight: 'I would
not exchange this one little English girl for the grand Turk's
whole seraglio; gazelle-eyes, houri forms and all!' It is perhaps a memory of Blanche in her oriental costume that stirs
in Jane's mind: 'The eastern allusion hit me again: "I'll not
stand you an inch in the stead of a seraglio," I said; "so don't
consider me an equivalent for one; if you have a fancy for
anything in that line, away with you, sir, to the bazaars of

Stamboul without delay; and lay out in extensive slave-purchases some of that spare cash you seem at a loss to spend satisfactorily here." ' [Chap. 24, II:242.] The relationship that Jane repudiates applies as well to Rochester's mistresses and to Bertha, of whom Jane has not heard at this point.

Blanche Ingram at Thornfield is everything that Bertha Mason appears to be before Rochester marries her. His father tells him that 'Miss Mason was the boast of Spanish Town for her beauty: and this was no lie. I found her a fine woman, in the style of Blanche Ingram; tall, dark, and majestic.' [Chap. 27, III:16.] Like Miss Ingram, she is un-English in appearance, for her Creole blood gives her a 'maroon' beauty resembling that of Caroline in *The Professor*. Her full sensual beauty, like that of Caroline, holds the promise of coarseness and future folly. 'I heard her lady-mother's character afterwards, and then I ceased to wonder at the precocious accomplishments of the daughter.' The words are Crimsworth's, describing Caroline, but they might be transferred intact to Rochester's account of Bertha. In a letter to Williams explaining her intentions for Bertha, Miss Brontë indicates the thematic and symbolic importance of the character: 'There is a phase of insanity which may be called moral madness. . . . Mrs. Rochester, indeed, lived a sinful life before she was insane, but sin is itself a species of insanity.' [Shorter, I:383–4.]

Miss Ratchford suggests that the prototype of Bertha Mason is Lady Zenobia Ellrington of the Angrian tales, particularly as she is described in 'Love and Jealousy'. Zenobia is a dark beauty whose face and figure are 'of a perfectly Roman cast', 'a bluestocking of deepest dye' given to fits of rage in which she kicks her victims downstairs, and in calmer moments fond of a few rounds of sparring, at which she is the equal of her husband, 'one of the best boxers on record'.[1] It is indicative of the association of Bertha and Blanche in Miss Brontë's mind that the description of Zenobia is as applic-

[1] Pp. 204–5.

able to Miss Ingram as it is to Mrs. Rochester.[1] In the novel Blanche and Bertha stand as symbols of licence, the one potential, the other realized: one as a warning to Jane, the other a revelation of the insane reality of unacknowledged sin, haunting and destroying attempts at a new life.

Georgiana is the embodiment in the novel of that recurring character of Miss Brontë's, the selfish, overblown blonde beauty who combines a passionate outlook and a lack of real emotion. As a child her pink cheeks and golden curls partially conceal 'a spoiled temper, a very acrid spite, a captious and insolent carriage'. [Chap. 2, 1:17.] Her favourite occupation is 'dressing her hair at the glass and interweaving her curls with artificial flowers and faded feathers'. [Chap. 4, 1:46.] 'Little darling!' cries the fervent Miss Abbot in unconscious revelation of the girl's character, 'with her long curls and her blue eyes, and such a sweet colour as she has; just as if she were painted!' [Chap. 3, 1:39.] Like Eulalie of Crimsworth's school, who is likened to a painted Madonna, Georgiana coarsens as she matures. When Jane returns to Gateshead, she finds 'a full-blown, very plump damsel, fair as wax-work; with handsome and regular features, languishing blue eyes, and ringleted yellow hair', [Chap. 21, 11:157] who also has the hard, ugly jaw she has inherited from her mother. 'Waxwork' and 'wax' are two of Miss Brontë's favourite words of disapproval in her description of beautiful women, indicating 'the ultimate insipidity of beauty of the senses alone. At her mother's death Georgiana bursts into loud weeping that is as unfeeling as her sister's total lack of demonstration.

[1] Bertha and Blanche resemble Zenobia in physical appearance and temper but not in accomplishments: it is quite as difficult to think of Bertha as a bluestocking as it is to imagine the Honourable Miss Ingram in pugilistic mood. Mrs. Rochester, who is a tall woman 'and corpulent besides', does, of course, grapple with her husband and is almost too powerful for him, since he is hampered in the struggle by not wishing to harm her. Miss Ingram in a similar emotional state might well prove too much for him, since she is a buxom 'strapper' and, if we are to judge by her prowess in riding, in far better fighting trim than Mrs. Rochester, whose diet seems confined to pudding and cheese, and whose exercise is restricted to an occasional nocturnal sprint through the corridors of Thornfield.

Such women as Georgiana are incapable of deep emotion, and after her failed elopement she secures her just reward in making 'an advantageous match with a wealthy worn-out man of fashion'. [Chap. 22, ii:186.]

Contrasted to the overemphatic beauty of Blanche and Georgiana, Adèle and Rosamond Oliver have the miniature charms of bloodless dolls and the triviality of the inhabitants of Lilliput. Adèle, good-natured, dainty, spoiled, elegant, of uncertain paternity, the product of an opera dancer's liaison, is an early version of the pretty daughter of Vale Hall. Her chief interest is in dress, her mind is immature for her age, and her playthings are constantly the waxen dolls that she resembles; Miss Ingram, with more insight than usual, says at the sight of her, 'Oh, what a little puppet!' [Chap. 17, ii:43.] Under Jane's guidance she becomes 'docile, good-tempered, and well-principled' as 'a sound, English education corrected in a great measure her French defects'. [Chap. 38, iii:306.] The kindness with which this illegitimate orphan is treated is in marked contrast to the treatment at Gateshead of Jane, Mrs. Reed's own connection.

Rosamond Oliver is the adult 'Peri' to which the 'puppet' Adèle might have grown (one wonders what the defects were in Rosamond's education, which was presumably English). She is the triumph of what came in a later day to be called 'chocolate-box' beauty, and she is described in terms so flat and trite as to indicate at once that her good looks go no deeper than the phrase implies: 'Perfect beauty is a strong expression; but I do not retract or qualify it: as sweet features as ever the temperate clime of Albion moulded; as pure hues of rose and lily as ever her humid gales and vapoury skies generated and screened, justified, in this instance, the term. No charm was wanting, no defect was perceptible: the young girl had regular and delicate lineaments: eyes shaped and coloured as we see them in lovely pictures, large, and dark, and full . . . white, smooth forehead . . . the lips fresh too, ruddy, healthy, sweetly formed; the even and gleaming teeth without flaw; the small, dimpled chin; the ornament of rich, plenteous tresses, – all advantages, in short, which combined, realize the ideal of beauty, were fully hers.' [Chap. 31, III: 126–7.] Her lack of emotional or intellectual maturity is indicated by her voice, which has 'a direct and naïve simplicity of tone and manner, pleasing, if child-like'. [Chap. 31, III: 128.] When disappointed in her flirtation with St. John, 'she would pout like a disappointed child; a pensive cloud would soften her radiant vivacity; she would withdraw her hand hastily from his, and turn in transient petulance'. [Chap. 32, III: 137.]

In taking to Jane with 'an amiable caprice', Miss Oliver gradually reveals 'her whole character; which was without mystery or disguise: she was coquettish, but not heartless; exacting, but not worthlessly selfish. She had been indulged from her birth, but was not absolutely spoilt. She was hasty, but good-humoured; vain (she could not help it, when every glance in the glass showed her such a flush of loveliness), but not affected; liberal-handed; innocent of the pride of wealth; ingenuous; sufficiently intelligent; gay, lively, and unthinking: she was very charming, in short, even to a cool observer of her own sex like me; but she was not profoundly interesting or thoroughly impressive. A very different sort of mind was hers from that, for instance, of the sisters of St. John. Still, I liked her almost as I liked my pupil Adèle; except that, for a child whom we have watched over and taught, a closer affection is engendered than we can give an equally attractive adult acquaintance.' [Chap. 32, III: 138–9.]

Beauty, save in the exceptional Rivers sisters, is seldom allied with character and intelligence. Mere physical attraction is not the mark of constancy, a loving nature, or even a very deep sexuality: Blanche quickly drops Rochester at the hint that the accounts of his fortune are exaggerated; Georgiana marries a 'worn-out man of fashion'; Rosamond within two months is engaged to a sprig of the local aristocracy. Jane calls St. John's attraction to Miss Oliver 'but a love of the senses' [Chap. 34, iii:188]; like other such bonds it quickly withers.

As a small girl Jane longs to be more flattered by her glass, but in her maturity she outgrows this essentially childish longing; the greatest adult pleasure she ever takes in her reflection is on the morning after Rochester's proposal, when she finds her face 'no longer plain'. [Chap. 24, ii:217.] Even when she is dressing to go to church with him to be married, she must be reminded by the maid to look at herself in the mirror: 'I saw a robed and veiled figure, so unlike my usual self that it seemed almost the image of a stranger.' [Chap. 26, ii:281.] It is dangerous to attach too much symbolic significance to random details in the novel, but it is tempting to feel that as Jane's self-knowledge increases, the reality of her reflected vision increases, and that the unfamiliar veiled figure in her glass is a reflection of the deceptive illusion of her expected marriage. Certainly, from this time forward she no longer seeks to see herself in the glass, as if she were at last certain of her own identity.

The fact that Blanche and Rosamond are the subjects of idealized portraits, and that Georgiana is as pretty 'as if she were painted', suggests an approach to Miss Brontë's curiously distrustful attitude to pictorial art in the novel. We know from Mrs. Gaskell that she spent a long period in her youth trying to learn to draw and paint in the Pre-Raphaelite manner, and on her trips to London much of her time was taken up with visits to the National Gallery, the Academy, and the major private collections in the city. In spite of this clear interest in pictures, she seems to have regarded them with something of the mixed fascination she felt for the Angrian creations of her youth, as something to be both loved and feared because they represented a kind of idealization that had little relation to truth. The pages of Bewick that Jane looks at as a child inspire romantic reverie, her own paintings at Lowood are of lurid seascapes, shipwrecks, corpses, apotheosized women, icebergs, and veiled heads with blank eyes and coronets of flame. 'I daresay you did exist in a kind of artist's dreamland while you blent and arranged these strange tints', [Chap. 13, 1:244–5] Rochester hazards without much fear of contradiction. Even the portrait of him that she draws at Gateshead is sketched almost automatically, in a kind of trance divorced from her rational volition, and is related to the other 'fancy vignettes' she draws at the same time from 'the ever-shifting kaleidoscope of imagination'. Reality is reflected only in her own severe self-portrait, sketched as a contrast to the head of Blanche, in order to quell her own rising love of Rochester; it is drawn as if looking into an unflattering glass, with no defect softened, no harsh line omitted, no irregularity smoothed away. Pictorial art, like theatricals and romantic fiction, is generally to be distrusted in the uncompromising search for reality.

When Williams asked Miss Brontë to illustrate the third edition of *Jane Eyre*, she wrote him in terms that indicate her belief that literature is a sterner art than its pictorial sister: 'I have, in my day, wasted a certain quantity of Bristol board and drawing-paper, crayons and cakes of colour, but when I examine the contents of my portfolio now, it seems as if during the years it has been lying closed some fairy had changed what I once thought sterling coin into dry leaves, and I feel much inclined to consign the whole collection of drawings to the fire; I see they have no value. If, then, *Jane Eyre* is ever to be illustrated, it must be by some other hand than that of its author. But I hope no one will be at the trouble to make portraits of my characters. Bulwer and Byron heroes and heroines are very well, they are all of them handsome; but my personages are mostly unattractive in looks, and therefore ill-adapted to figure in ideal portraits.' [Shorter, 1:401–2.]

Fortunately, her own imperfectly mastered attraction towards the stuff that dreams are made on persists in the novel in constant balance with her stern desire for a naked objectivity, and it is the eternal tension between them that gives the book such a special flavour. The danger of over-reliance upon either the subjective or the objective, the equal peril of ignoring either: these themes so animated Miss Brontë's imagination that the result is one of the finest achievements of the romantic sensibility.

3

SHIRLEY

'Something real, cool, and solid, lies before you,' wrote Charlotte Brontë in the opening of *Shirley*; 'something unromantic as Monday morning.' In denying the reader a promise of 'sentiment, and poetry, and reverie', 'passion, and stimulus, and melodrama', [Chap. 1, 1:1–2] she was somewhat disingenuous, although it is true that there is a good deal less 'poetry' than readers of *Jane Eyre* probably expected of her next novel. But of sentiment, reverie, passion, melodrama, and stimulus (whatever she meant by that term) there is more, to be honest, than most readers can stomach. God's plenty, one might say if Deity were more important in this novel.

As in *The Professor*, Miss Brontë's formal allegiance is to a disciplined novel, with both her own emotions and those of her characters kept in firm check; it is no surprise that her absorption with the non-rational aspects of life threatens to wreck the unity of the novel by fighting against the rational impulses that she is avowedly supporting. Again and again, we see her poised on the edge of unleashing the torrent of emotive force of *Jane Eyre*, then prudently drawing back. A small but illustrative example is her description of Shirley's house, looking like a Girtin water-colour: 'If Fieldhead had few other merits as a building, it might at least be termed picturesque: its irregular architecture, and the grey and mossy colouring communicated by time, gave it a just claim to this epithet. The old latticed windows, the stone porch, the walls, the roof, the chimney-stacks, were rich in crayon touches and sepia lights and shades. The trees behind were fine, bold, and spreading; the cedar on the lawn in front was grand, and the granite urns on the garden wall, the fretted arch of the gateway, were, for an artist, as the very desire of the eye.' [Chap. 11, 1:276–7.]

The setting is that of a Gothic novel, but when we are taken inside, we find that instead of developing the air of mystery the narrator treats us to a disquisition on the difficulties of spring-cleaning the panelling in this 'gothic old barrack': 'Whoever, having the bowels of humanity, has seen servants scrubbing at these polished wooden walls with bees-waxed cloths on a warm May day, must allow that they are "[in]tolerable and not to be endured"; and I cannot but secretly applaud the benevolent barbarian who had painted another and larger apartment of Fieldhead—the drawing-room to-wit, formerly also an oak-room—of a delicate pinky white; thereby earning for himself the character of a Hun, but mightily enhancing the cheerfulness of that portion of his abode, and saving future housemaids a world of toil.' [Chap. 11, 1:289.] With a rude wrench, we are back in the literally workaday world. Fieldhead shelters no ghosts, and its inhabitant is a most level-headed, unmysterious person.

Twice Caroline Helstone sees 'apparitions' in the moonlight, but, unromantically enough, they turn out to be only her friends walking in the evening air. On another occasion Robert sees her form in his cottage parlour when he knows that she cannot be there, but her dress and face dissolve into 'the sweep of a white muslin curtain, and a balsam-plant in a flower-pot'. [Chap. 13, 11:68.]

Caroline suffers a long illness that is obviously her hypochondriac reaction to disappointed love, but we are told bluntly that no one ever dies 'of love or grief alone; though some die of inherent maladies, which the tortures of those passions prematurely force into destructive action. . . . The blossom which the March wind nips, but fails to sweep away, may survive to hang a withered apple on the tree late into autumn: having braved the last frosts of spring, it may also brave the first of winter.' [Chap. 11, I:283.]

Shirley, too, is thought to be on the brink of death, but she finally reveals that her wasting away is due to fear of hydrophobia from a dog's bite: certainly a sufficient cause for worry but hardly what the reader of romantic fiction expects, and the matter is dropped with the assurance 'that in her case the bite proved innocuous'. [Chap. 36, III:266.] Both Moores suffer illnesses that affect their psyches, but their prosaic causes are Robert's gunshot wound and the fever that Louis had 'perhaps caught . . . in one of the poor cottages of the district'. [Chap. 27, III:84.] When Louis suggests emigration to the wild West, he declares that he would rather behold Nature through 'the soft human eyes of a loved and lovely wife, than through the wild orbs of the highest goddess of Olympus'. Shirley cuts through the thicket of verbiage with the practical reminder that 'Juno could not cook a buffalo steak as you like it'. [Chap. 36, III:274.]

Miss Brontë's frequent undercutting of romantic attitudes is some indication of their importance to her, for all her protestations of the Monday mornings of the novel. Her outburst at being unable to complete the story of Malone is a reminder of how much more deeply she was committed to the reality of imagination, large emotion, fate, and coincidence than she was to the prosaic, the probable, and the mundane: 'Were I to give the catastrophe of your life and conversation, the public would sweep off in shrieking hysterics, and there would be a wild cry for sal-volatile and burnt feathers. "Impossible!" would be pronounced here: "untrue!" would be responded there. "Inartistic!" would be solemnly decided. Note well! Whenever you present the actual, simple truth, it is, somehow, always denounced as a lie: they disown it, cast it off, throw it on the parish; whereas the product of your own imagination, the mere figment, the sheer fiction, is adopted, petted, termed pretty, proper, sweetly natural: the little, spurious wretch gets all the comfits,—the honest, lawful bantling, all the cuffs. Such is the way of the world, Peter; and, as you are the legitimate urchin, rude, unwashed, and naughty, you must stand down.' [Chap. 37, III:297–8.] Curiously, though not uncharacteristically, she is equating fiction with the prosaic, truth with the unbelievable.

Since all of Miss Brontë's novels are at least partly auto-biographical, the problem of the relationship between fact and fiction was one that frequently occupied her, and it is a problem to which she never found a satisfactory, or even constant, answer. The passage just quoted from the end of *Shirley* shows her belief in a non-rational reality that transcends fact, but her creation of character sometimes seems a contradiction of this belief. The Yorke family, who might be described as the major secondary characters of the novel, were drawn directly from life, the models being a Yorkshire manufacturer and his family with whom Miss Brontë was acquainted, and so closely do the Yorkes resemble their originals that many of the author's friends instantly recognized them under their new names. Miss Brontë's answer to Ellen Nussey, quoted earlier, about the identity of originals in the novel is adequate answer to the problem of whether she was attempting to reproduce events from her own experience in faithful detail and to draw literal portraits of those she knew: 'It would not suit the rules of art, nor my own feelings, to write in that style. We only suffer reality to *suggest*, never to *dictate*. The heroines are abstractions, and the heroes also. Qualities I have seen, loved, and admired, are here and there put in as decorative gems, to be preserved in that setting.' Her intent is clear, her practice another matter.

Subsidiary characters and events may serve any of several functions in a novel: they may be necessary to move the action, and they may provide analogues to the main characters and events or a viewpoint from which to consider them. They may also, as critics too often forget, exist simply for the pleasure they provide in themselves. Who, for instance, would wish to sacrifice the delicious scene of Mr. Pickwick sliding gravely on the ice, falling on his capacious posterior, and, when at last his weight proves too great, vanishing with dignity into the chilly water? The scene does not take the action forward, nor does it tell us anything of that great man that we do not already know, but our pleasure in the book would be less without it.

Yorke provides some of this latter kind of pleasure, as he deliberately shifts from fluent French and standard English into his native Doric when he is 'setting down' someone. Throughout the book he also acts as counsellor to Robert Moore, attempting to inculcate in him the rational, unsentimental views that have taken root but imperfectly in his own mind. Mrs. Yorke stands as an example of the hardness into which self-reliance may grow. Martin Yorke acts as a male reflector of Caroline's excessive sensibility, although he would stoutly deny it, and Rose is perhaps useful in enunciating the claims of the world upon women kept only as household drudges. Of these members of the family Miss Brontë makes adequate employment, but the other members, Matthew, Mark, and Jessy, act as red herrings, promising, by their careful description, to become important in the progress of the novel, and then never fulfilling the reader's expectations. Twice we are told of Jessy's death in years to come in a foreign land, where she is buried among strangers, 'cold, coffined, solitary—only the sod screening her from the storm'. [Chap. 23, ii:297.] The reason for Miss Brontë's descriptions of the futures of Matthew, Mark, and Jessy seems primarily to be that the originals of these characters were part of the family from which the Yorkes were drawn, and that consequently she felt she must include them and tell all that she knew about them.[1] As characters they hardly exist, for they neither contribute to the major themes and actions of the book nor provide pleasure in themselves. Miss

[1] Probably the recent loss of her brother and sisters made Miss Brontë feel that the death of Jessy was more significant than it is for the reader.

Brontë has mistaken the literal for the significant. The Yorkes might stand in small for all the characters and actions in the novel that seem put in to fill out a panorama rather than because of their importance. The digressions are primarily responsible for the feeling of the reader that the book is too long for its contents. This irrelevant material is particularly noticeable because *Shirley* falls between *Jane Eyre* and *Villette*, in both of which Miss Brontë pruned extraneous matter and managed to give significance to the autobiographical matter that she employed. We know that the personal difficulties under which she wrote the book made her doubt her abilities; they may also have kept her from seeing her own irrelevancies.

The world of *Jane Eyre* is one of portents, spiritual immanence, and mystery, and Mrs. Rochester seems no more improbable an inhabitant of Thornfield than Mrs. Fairfax. When an active Providence constantly intervenes in the world, when symbol is more important than cold fact, one is more ready to accept exaggerated emotion, passionate monologues, melodramatic thrills, and even bombastic speech.

But Briarfield and Thornfield have little in common save a similarity in name. All the action of *Shirley* takes place within the careful described confines of Mr. Helstone's parish or its immediate neighbourhood, and characters who go further afield than Nunnely Priory simply drop out of the story until their return to the circumscribed pocket of Yorkshire that is the centre of the story. It is a locale of painstaking realism with its roots in the *Annual Register* rather than in the Gothic tale. There are actual working-men speaking broad Yorkshire as they dye cotton or lose their jobs, landladies worry about their rent, country visiting is accompanied by slices of ham (nowhere else in Miss Brontë's pages is there so much description of food), the number of shillings needed to save out-of-work labourers from starvation is carefully calculated, preserves burn when molasses is used instead of sugar. Against such a background of Monday morning, outsize

emotions and inflated rhetoric loom in fustian, and the moon
is suddenly seen to be made of country cheese.

The world in which Jane Eyre lives is presided over by a
supernatural power that steps in to provide the heroine with
family, fortune, and finally a husband, a power that is in such
close connection with men that chestnut trees writhe at their
impiety. If there is a presiding god in *Shirley*, it is the shining
golden power of money, frustrating those who are deprived
of it, keeping them from love and human companionship,
even confining its possessors behind a barrier that frightens
off intruders into their isolation. The love of Caroline and
Robert Moore can come to fruition only when the wheels of
the cotton mills recommence their satanic revolutions after
the repeal of the Orders in Council, men fight and die to
divert their masters' sovereigns into their own pockets,
marriages are arranged to consolidate fortunes, and women
without dowries eke out miserable lives as old maids. Robert
pockets his own decency and asks Shirley not for her hand
but her purse. Louis is as impressed as Robert by her fortune
and nearly loses her through inability to understand that a
woman may have both £1,000 a year and an independent
heart. And Shirley herself takes more spontaneous pleasure
in her profits than she does in the charity that she so dutifully
disperses. It is frequently a hard, cold world, one in which
the avaricious Eliza Reed would not be out of place, and one
where fulness of emotion is the exception not the ruling principle of men's lives.

In no other novel of Charlotte Brontë is there so much talk
of churches, parish schools, clergymen, and the religious
affiliations of characters, and in no other is there so little
sense of Christianity having any effect upon its adherents.
The curates drink too much, scheme for advantageous marriage, abuse the Dissenters, pick over 'minute points of
ecclesiastical discipline, frivolities which seemed empty as
bubbles to all save themselves'; 'theology they may discuss
occasionally, but piety—never.' [Chap. 1, 1:7, 4.] Caroline

prays for relief of her loneliness and meets Martin at church for clandestine news of Robert, but otherwise takes only the conventional interest in religion proper to the Rector's niece. The Moores (perhaps because they are half-Belgian) pay scant attention to religion, and Shirley is frankly pagan, in spite of her formal connection with parish affairs as chief local landowner. Mr. Helstone is a spoiled soldier more interested in a good fight than in the spiritual welfare of his parish. Dr. Boultby rumbles pious platitudes from the depths of a well-filled belly, and only Mr. Hall seems to have any sense of being the heir of St. Peter, although Miss Brontë suggests that the devotion of his feminine parishioners is as attributable to his celibate state as to his sanctity. 'It was a joyous scene, and a scene to do good,' she writes of the school-feast procession, led by the three rectors: 'it was a day of happiness for rich and poor; the work, first, of God, and then of the clergy. Let England's priests have their due: they are a faulty set in some respects, being only of common flesh and blood, like us all; but the land would be badly off without them: Britain would miss her church, if that church fell. God save it! God also reform it!' [Chap. 16, II:136.]

The satiric tone of the last words is underlined by the meeting of the newly formed procession and a rival band of the 'Dissenting and Methodist schools, the Baptists, Independents, and Wesleyans, joined in unholy alliance'. [Chap. 17, II:139–40.] When the two processions meet in a narrow lane, the superior force of the Churchmen and the noise of their massed bands rout the Nonconformists, who retreat in alarm, leaving their own leader thrown into a ditch. 'Rule, Britannia' has drowned the singing of psalms, but one wonders whether there is much to choose between arrogant force and impudent drunkenness.

Miss Brontë's biographers have frequently pointed out that Branwell, Emily, and Anne all died during the period that she was writing *Shirley*, and that their deaths greatly affected the novel. When Caroline is apparently dying, Mrs. Pryor, usually so docile, changes from supplication to demand for her daughter's life. 'Till break of day, she wrestled with God in earnest prayer.' With obvious reference to the events of her own life, Miss Brontë begins the next chapter: 'Not always do those who dare such divine conflict prevail. Night after night the sweat of agony may burst dark on the forehead; the supplicant may cry for mercy with that soundless voice the soul utters when its appeal is to the Invisible. "Spare my beloved," it may implore. "Heal my life's life. Rend not from me what long affection entwines with my whole nature. God of heaven—bend—hear—be clement!" And after this cry and strife, the sun may rise and see him worsted. That opening morn, which used to salute him with the whisper of zephyrs, the carol of skylarks, may breathe, as its first accents, from the dear lips which colour and heat have quitted,—

' "Oh! I have had a suffering night. This morning I am worse. I have tried to rise. I cannot. Dreams I am unused to have troubled me."

'Then the watcher approaches the patient's pillow, and sees a new and strange moulding of the familiar features, feels at once that the insufferable moment draws nigh, knows that it is God's will his idol shall be broken, and bends his head, and subdues his soul to the sentence he cannot avert, and scarce can bear.' [Chap. 25, III:31–2.] Caroline's recovery seems the careless gift of a capricious Providence.

To find religion without temporal meaning and comfort would not be surprising in a twentieth-century novel, nor would it seem noteworthy here had not Miss Brontë so saturated *The Professor* and *Jane Eyre* with the sense of divine comfort as a necessary consequence in this life to man's tribulations.

That Miss Brontë's religious faith was not completely gone, we know from her letter to W. S. Williams on 13 June 1849: 'Had I never believed in a future life before, my sisters' fate would assure me of it. There must be Heaven or

we must despair—for life seems bitter, brief—blank. To me—
these two have left in their memories a noble legacy.
. . . there is something in the past I can love intensely and
honour deeply—and it is something which cannot change—
which cannot decay—which immortality guarantees from corruption.' [*SHB*, ii:339–40.] A belief in personal immortality is quite different, however, from an abiding sense of
divine immanence, and from this time forward, Miss Brontë's
work is full of the awareness of the bitterness, the brevity,
and the blankness of life. It is an awareness that is hardly
tempered in this novel by joy in the hope of heaven.

Whether or not the change came about as a result of the
deaths of her sisters and brother, *Shirley* marks a watershed
in Miss Brontë's novels. It has been customary to group *The
Professor* and *Shirley* as examples of an attempt at realism in
the novel, with *Jane Eyre* and *Villette* as triumphs of the
imagination. It would be equally valid to speak of her first
two novels as exemplifying Miss Brontë's early optimism
and hope, with *Shirley* showing her growing doubt and
pessimism, followed by the autumnal resignation of earthly
hope in *Villette*. The distinct darkening in her outlook is
probably responsible for the general preference of readers
for *The Professor* to *Shirley*, and the greater popularity of
Jane Eyre over that of *Villette*, although the latter novel in
each pair is the more skilful technically.

In the conventional sense, *Shirley* has a 'happy' ending,
with the four major characters united in marriages of reasonable financial stability, but the wedding bells hardly drown
our memory of the loveless marriages of Helstone, Mrs.
Pryor, and Yorke, or of the lonely spinsters of the parish.
Nor do they vitiate the dark effect of the illnesses of Caroline,
Shirley, Louis, and Robert, the mutual hatred of workman
and employer, the midnight murders, and the wounded men
writhing and moaning in the dust outside the mill as the summer sun rises after a night of terror. No wonder that Caroline's visions of an untroubled life of love seem enchanted

'dream-scenes', the illusions of eighteen, when 'Elf-land lies behind us, the shores of Reality rise in front'. 'Every joy that life gives must be earned ere it is secured; and how hardly earned, those only know who have wrestled for great prizes. The heart's blood must gem with red beads the brow of the combatant, before the wreath of victory rustles over it.' [Chap. 7, 1:135–6.]

Caroline begins to reach the shores of reality when she first realizes that Robert's affectionate manner holds no promise for the future. In one of the personal outbursts that occasionally shatter the thin veneer of fiction in the novel, Miss Brontë transfers her own passionate disillusion to Caroline. It is, she tells us, 'not germane to Caroline Helstone's feelings', but its violently intrusive tone indicates how deeply the author felt when writing *Shirley*: 'Take the matter as you find it: ask no questions; utter no remonstrances: it is your best wisdom. You expected bread, and you have got a stone; break your teeth on it, and don't shriek because the nerves are martyrized: do not doubt that your mental stomach—if you have such a thing—is strong as an ostrich's—the stone will digest. You held out your hand for an egg, and fate put into it a scorpion. Show no consternation: close your fingers firmly upon the gift; let it sting through your palm. Never mind: in time, after your hand and arm have swelled and quivered long with torture, the squeezed·scorpion will die, and you will have learned the great lesson how to endure without a sob. For the whole remnant of your life, if you survive the test—some, it is said, die under it—you will be stronger, wiser, less sensitive. This you are not aware of, perhaps, at the time, and so cannot borrow courage of that hope.' [Chap, 7, 1:147.]

The difference between this stoic acceptance of one's pain and isolation in life, and the simpler self-reliance demanded of Jane Eyre to sustain her through temporary and temporal vicissitudes is an indication of how deeply Miss Brontë's outlook had changed in a year or two. The new attitude is still further from the statement in *The Professor* that 'if we rarely taste the fulness of joy in this life, we yet more rarely savour the acrid bitterness of hopeless anguish'.

Presumably with the intention of supplying the objectivity consonant with Monday mornings, in *Shirley*, Miss Brontë made her only full-length attempt at narration primarily in the third person; as a method, it is considerably less successful than the first-person narrations of the central characters of the other novels. Miss Brontë alternates between the employment of what are known, in Professor Booth's useful phrase, as dramatized and undramatized narrators.[1] Usually we are unaware of the impersonal narrator, but occasionally, primarily in her setting the time of the action, there is a hint of personality and direct involvement on her part. (The narrator must not be confused with the author herself, of course, however much alike their reactions may be; it is, for example, manifestly impossible for Miss Brontë to have been personally involved in the events of 1812 that form the background of the novel. Nor are their perceptions always intended to be identical. In this limited sense, the narrator is as much the author's creation as is any other character in the novel.) There is no purpose in beating an author of the mid-nineteenth century with criteria primarily applicable to the novels of Henry James and his successors; all the same, one feels that there is either too little or too much detachment on the part of the narrator. In a number of places throughout the novel, the narrator speaks in the authorial voice as 'I', with a consequent shock to the reader, who has forgotten that the novel is not totally related by an impersonal narrator, and who has been undisturbed by the revelation of actions and emotions that no human being could reasonably be aware of, aside from the character involved. It seems at least probable that Miss Brontë was influenced in *Shirley* by the example set by her master, Thackeray, in *Vanity Fair*, which

---

[1] Wayne C. Booth, *The Rhetoric of Fiction* (University of Chicago Press, Chicago, 1961), p. 151.

appeared in the interval between *Jane Eyre* and *Shirley*. The Olympian magician of Thackeray's novel frankly confesses to dangling his characters before our eyes like so many puppets, but we accept his authorial intrusions as master puppeteer because he so openly proclaims that his plot is an act of illusion, and because his manipulations are undertaken with the detachment of the comic spirit, pouring peals of silvery laughter over the follies of the world. The ultimate reality of his great novel becomes the view point of the urbane and wry, but warm-hearted, observer of man's foibles.

In *Shirley*, Miss Brontë is seldom detached from the reactions of her characters, and her intention is certainly not comic, even in the broadest meaning of that term, save perhaps in the case of Caroline, who is clearly intended to be viewed objectively in her over-romantic reactions to the neglect of Robert Moore. Since there is no particular use made of a discrepancy between the viewpoint of the author and that of the characters, the occasional reminder of the narrator's presence serves more as a distraction than as a guide to the meaning of the novel. Whereas Thackeray, as narrator, becomes the most important single voice of *Vanity Fair*, Miss Brontë's role as narrator is negligible and no clear impression of the narrator's personality emerges.

Probably at one moment only in the novel does Miss Brontë use the point of view of the narrator clearly and forcefully. In the closing paragraphs, the narrator re-establishes the fact that nearly forty years have elapsed since the major action, and then her old housekeeper tells of the Hollow as it had been in 1812: 'Different to what it is now; but I can tell of it clean different again: when there was neither mill, nor cot, nor hall, except Fieldhead, within two miles of it. I can tell, one summer-evening, fifty years syne, my mother coming running in just at the edge of dark, almost fleyed out of her wits, saying, she had seen a fairish (fairy) in Fieldhead Hollow; and that was the last fairish that ever was seen on this country side (though they've been heard within these forty years). A lonesome spot it was–and a bonnie spot –full of oak trees and nut trees. It is altered now.' [Chap. 37, III:316–17.] In the last two sentences lie all the lament for the Yorkshire that antedated the Industrial Revolution, as well as the acceptance that the earth turns and the world changes. It is probably not an important effect, but it is one that could be achieved only by the use of a narrator who is involved sympathetically with the action.[1]

In *Jane Eyre* the character of Jane herself, capricious, changeable, and sometimes inconsistent, helps maintain a unity of tone as the action is filtered through her mind, her imagination and memory. The sensibility of the novel is Jane's own, and what might be jarring contradictions are resolved as disparate aspects of her humanly variable perceptions. Too much reliance on rationality, for instance, is as much a part of the formation of her character as is the over-dependence upon emotion. In *Shirley*, Miss Brontë is once more concerned with the old tug-of-war between rationality and the emotions, but almost as if she were aware of the difficulties of presenting this kind of divided sensibility except as it is embodied in separate characters, she splits the consciousness that Jane represents into two parts, assigning that of the too-romantic young girl to Caroline, that of the tougher, more rational woman to Shirley. The effect is reminiscent of *Sense and Sensibility*, although Miss Brontë had, of course, never read Jane Austen's novel.[2] In *Jane Eyre* the interest is primarily in one character as she alternates between Gateshead and Lowood, between Rochester and St. John; in *Shirley* the central character changes as the narrator's attention switches.

[1] The housekeeper is, to be sure, not the narrator of the novel; although the speech is hers, the effect is dependent upon the presence of the narrator, who has gone through the whole plot with us.

[2] In the same way, Jane and Rochester remind us, in their learning to 'suit' one another, of Elizabeth and the well-born D'Arcy going through the same process in *Pride and Prejudice*. Miss Brontë probably had more in common with her great predecessor than she was aware of.

Despite the title of the novel, Caroline Helstone holds the stage for a much larger portion of the book than does Shirley, who does not come into the novel until it is one-third over. Caroline is the first pretty heroine of one of Miss Brontë's novels. To the reader who knows *Jane Eyre*, the first description of Caroline may seem vaguely familiar:

'To her had not been denied the gift of beauty; it was not absolutely necessary to know her in order to like her; she was fair enough to please, even at the first view. Her shape suited her age; it was girlish, light, and pliant; every curve was neat, every limb proportionate: her face was expressive and gentle; her eyes were handsome, and gifted at times with a winning beam that stole into the heart, with a language that spoke softly to the affections. Her mouth was very pretty; she had a delicate skin, and a fine flow of brown hair, which she knew how to arrange with taste; curls became her, and she possessed them in picturesque profusion. Her style of dress announced taste in the wearer; very unobtrusive in fashion, far from costly in material, but suitable in colour to the fair complexion with which it contrasted, and in make to the slight form which it draped.' [Chap. 6, 1:104–5.]

The sense of familiarity in the passage derives from the reminiscence of the description of Rosamond Oliver (see pp. 104–5). It would be unfair to Miss Brontë's flexibility to assume that a physical likeness between her characters must necessarily mean that they fulfil the same function. All the same, the praise is in highly conventional terms of mere prettiness, a quality for which she had little use, and it is no shock when she finishes the description in words that are, at best, equivocal: 'So much for Caroline Helstone's appearance; as to her character or intellect, if she had any, they must speak for themselves in due time.' [Chap. 6, 1:105.]

Caroline appealed greatly to Miss Brontë's contemporary readers, as well she might, for she is the epitome of the popular idea of the Victorian 'heroine': pretty, sweet, gentle, retiring, trembling at a frown, and with no particular gifts of intellect. With a change of clothes and name, she might double for any of a dozen *ingénues* in unimportant novels of the period, or, more importantly, as Dora Spenlow or Amelia Sedley. Like Dickens and Thackeray, Miss Brontë clearly regarded the child-woman with a mixture of affection and annoyance, and like them, she attempted to project both aspects of her ambivalent attitude. She is, however, even harder on frailty in her own sex than the two male writers are. Into Caroline she poured all her sympathy for a woman condemned by circumstance to have neither education nor intellect, and in her she found all that she disliked in a conventional girl of little spirit. Caroline, like Dora and Amelia, was loved by contemporaries who failed to see how far from complete her creator's admiration was; with an equal lack of subtlety later generations have condemned all three young ladies as sentimental, mistaking the sentimentality of the character for that of the author.

'If men could see us as we really are, they would be a little amazed,' Shirley says in irritation; 'but the cleverest, the acutest men are often under an illusion about women: they do not read them in a true light; they misapprehend them, both for good and evil: their good woman is a queer thing, half doll, half angel; their bad woman almost always a fiend. Then to hear them fall into extasies with each other's creations, worshipping the heroine of such a poem–novel– drama, thinking it fine–divine! Fine and divine it may be, but often quite artificial–false as the rose in my best bonnet there. If I spoke all I think on this point; if I gave my real opinion of some first-rate female characters in first-rate works, where should I be? Dead under a cairn of avenging stones in half an hour.' [Chap. 20, ii:209–10.]

Caroline's lack of spirit is underlined by Yorke's comparison of her pallid stillness to one of the works of that most passive of sculptors, Canova. [Chap. 30, iii:171.] She is, Shirley tells Moore, feminine to a degree, 'nor of what they call the spirited order of women', a girl whose rare outbursts have no 'manly fire', but only 'a short, vivid, trembling glow, that shot up, shone, vanished' and 'left her scared at her own daring'. [Chap. 20, ii:226.]

When Caroline believes that Robert no longer loves her, she begins to decline in physical and spiritual tone. 'Robert had done her no wrong: he had told her no lie; it was she that was to blame, if any one was: what bitterness her mind distilled should and would be poured on her own head. She had loved without being asked to love,–a natural, some-times an inevitable chance, but big with misery.' [Chap. 7, i:149.] In her hypochondriacal state, which, as always, is equated with superstition, she longs to leave the Rectory, where 'it is said that the out-kitchens . . . were once en-closed in the churchyard, and that there are graves under them.' 'I think I grow what is called nervous,' she tells Mrs. Pryor. 'I see things under a darker aspect than I used to do. I have fears I never used to have–not of ghosts, but of omens and disastrous events; and I have an inexpressible weight on my mind which I would give the world to shake off, and I cannot do it.' 'Strange!' cries the healthy-minded Shirley, free at the time of both superstition and excess emotionalism. 'I never feel so.' [Chap. 13, ii:46–7.]

In the tradition of deserted maidens, Caroline, unable to sleep for unrequited love, spends the night in waking dreams of Robert: 'as dawn approached, the setting stars and break-ing day dimmed the creation of Fancy'. [Chap. 13, ii:74.] 'Fancy' is the clue to Caroline's position in the novel; in a world of Monday mornings, she exists in a land of visions, unconnected to the earth, walking like a phantom through the night-haunted wood, brooding over the Mill where Robert works, loitering in the wood outside the Yorke house like a Victorian Oenone longing for the sight of her Paris, blending mysteriously into Martin Yorke's fairy tales, like the wood nymph for which he takes her. As Jane Eyre did at Gateshead, she lives in a world of childhood fantasy. Unlike Shirley, an omnivorous reader, Caroline rejects the

sterner pleasures of Racine and Corneille, whom Mlle.
Moore so admires, and whispers to herself the romantic
poetry of Chénier in French, and the poetry of the tormented
Cowper in her own tongue. Only when she is transformed by
the presence of Robert can she revive herself from self
absorption and read Shakespeare's comic scenes 'with a spirit
no one could have expected of her, with a pithy expression
with which she seemed gifted on the spot, and for that brief
moment only'. [Chap. 6, I:128.]

Employing her usual method of characterization by literary
taste, Miss Brontë sketches in the quality of Caroline's mind
when she sits alone, 'still as a garden statue,' reading old
books 'taken from her uncle's library: the Greek and Latin
were of no use to her; and its collection of light literature was
chiefly contained on a shelf which had belonged to her aunt
Mary: some venerable Lady's Magazines, that had once
performed a sea voyage with their owner, and undergone a
storm, and whose pages were stained with salt water; some
mad Methodist Magazines, full of miracles and apparitions,
of preternatural warnings, ominous dreams, and frenzied
fanaticism; the equally mad Letters of Mrs. Elizabeth Rowe
from the Dead to the Living; a few old English Classics:—
from these faded flowers Caroline had in her childhood ex-
tracted the honey,—they were tasteless to her now.' [Chap.
22, II:268–9.]

In contrast to the shrinking femininity of Caroline is Shirley Keeldar, who is in many respects aggressively masculine.
The polarity of the two girls is suggested by Shirley's first
attraction to Caroline 'because she was quiet, retiring,
looked delicate, and seemed as if she needed some one to take
care of her'. [Chap. 12, II:23.] Given a boy's name at birth,
Shirley has grown into man's estate as lord of the manor,
supervisor of her own farm, owner of the mill ('The counting-house is better than my bloom-coloured drawing-room:
I adore the counting-house.' [Chap. 11, I:302]), and, as
Mr. Sympson finds out to his discomfiture, head of the

family. 'I am indeed no longer a girl, but quite a woman, and something more,' she says in triumph to the Rector. 'I am an esquire: Shirley Keeldar, Esquire, ought to be my style and title. They gave me a man's name; I hold a man's position: it is enough to inspire me with a touch of manhood. . . . You must choose me for your churchwarden, Mr. Helstone, the next time you elect new ones: they ought to make me a magistrate and a captain of yeomanry: Tony Lumpkin's mother was a colonel, and his aunt a justice of the peace—why shouldn't I be?' [Chap. 11, 1:298–9].

Shirley loves to talk business, she stands at her fire with her hands held behind her back, she rides alone across the moors, taking the descents as fast as her horse will go, she sings with unladylike expression, and she whistles, to the dismay of Mrs. Pryor, who reproves her for her habits: 'My dear, do not allow that habit of alluding to yourself as a gentleman to be confirmed: it is a strange one. Those who do not know you, hearing you speak thus, would think you affected masculine manners.' [Chap. 12, II:2.]

Like the captain whose rank she confers on herself, she has a martial spirit that inflames with any hint of resistance. 'Bad manners!' she says of the Dissenters who are pushed into the ditch when they obstruct the school procession, 'and I hate bad manners. Of course, they must have a lesson.' [Chap. 17, II:140.] At the threat of danger to her property, she becomes as dangerous as her idol, Wellington: 'For, after all, if political incendiaries come here to kindle conflagration in the neighbourhood, and my property is attacked, I shall defend it like a tigress—I know I shall. Let me listen to Mercy as long as she is near me: her voice once drowned by the shout of ruffian defiance, and I shall be full of impulses to resist and quell. If once the poor gather and rise in the form of the mob, I shall turn against them as an aristocrat: if they bully me, I must defy; if they attack, I must resist,—and I will.' [Chap. 14, II:85–6.]

Yet, for all her assumed masculinity, Shirley is no feminist, nor does she want to dominate a lover or husband. Man, she tells Caroline, who agrees only too readily, 'is a noble being. I tell you when they *are* good, they are the lords of creation,— they are the sons of God. Moulded in their Maker's image, the minutest spark of His spirit lifts them almost above mortality. Indisputably, a great, good, handsome man is the first of created things. . . . Nothing ever charms me more than when I meet my superior—one who makes me sincerely feel that he is my superior.' [Chap. 12, II:15–16.]

Unlike Caroline, she will not allow her pride and self-respect to be humbled by easy mastery, and when she has finally admitted her love for Louis, she warns him that she will preserve her independent nature, that she can be mastered but never tamed. Like Millamant in the great proviso scene in *The Way of the World*, she battles to the last in defence of a freedom that she is anxious to lose, and finally consents to dwindle by slow degrees into a woman and wife. Convinced at last that she and Louis are completely equal (as Jane Eyre held herself and Rochester to be), she refuses to acknowledge that money has any power where love is concerned, and asks only to stay in the loving relationship of pupil to Louis as master: ' "Mr. Moore," said she, looking up with a sweet, open, earnest countenance, "teach me and help me to be good. I do not ask you to take off my shoulders all the cares and duties of property; but I ask you to share the burden, and to show me how to sustain my part well. Your judgment is well-balanced; your heart is kind; your principles are sound. I know you are wise; I feel you are benevolent; I believe you are conscientious. Be my companion through life; be my guide where I am ignorant; be my master where I am faulty; be my friend always!" ' [Chap. 36, III: 286–7.] Submission does not come easily, and at the prospect of losing her total freedom, she gnaws at her chain, like the leopardess to which Louis compares her, and tries to escape the impending marriage until Louis forces her to name a date.

Shirley, we know from Mrs. Gaskell, was Charlotte Brontë's portrait of her sister Emily, 'had she been placed in health and prosperity', and into the character Miss Brontë put all the love—and perhaps the bafflement—that she felt for that enigmatic genius. The title of the book is indicative of the importance that Shirley was meant to assume in spite of the infrequency of her appearances in the plot, for Miss Brontë told Williams that she 'has turned out the most prominent and peculiar character in the work'. [Shorter, II:65.] The only trouble, as Miss Phyllis Bentley has written,[1] is that there is really no action in the book sufficient to realize the potentialities of this splendidly emancipated young woman.

The emancipation of woman from mere conventionality is a theme that occupies Miss Brontë in all her novels, but nowhere else is it so important as in *Shirley*. Indeed, it would be difficult to think of any other major fictional works before Shaw's plays (except the novels of Meredith) in which the problem is so central. The contrast between the modern woman and the womanly woman is made continuously throughout the novel, a half-century before Ann Whitfield first stepped on the stage.

Caroline is, 'compared with the heiress, as a graceful pencil-sketch compared with a vivid painting'. [Chap. 13, II:60.] In the chapter called 'Two Lives' the first picture is of Shirley at Fieldhead: 'How does she look? Like a love-lorn maiden, pale and pining for a neglectful swain? Does she sit the day long bent over some sedentary task? Has she for ever a book in her hand, or sewing on her knee, and eyes only for that, and words for nothing, and thoughts unspoken? By no means. Shirley is all right.' [Chap. 22, II:261.] Instead of working for the hated Jew-basket, Shirley occupies herself happily—and even somewhat usefully—around the house and farm, then throws herself on the floor to read single-mindedly. While she is so employed, Caroline moons about the Rectory

---

[1] *The Brontës* (Home and Van Thal, London, 1947), p. 74.

garden, bored and wondering how Miss Ainsley 'managed to be so equably serene in *her* solitude'. [Chap. 22, ii:269.] The simple fact that Miss Ainsley is not totally self-absorbed never occurs to her. In the closing of the chapter Caroline has a long interior monologue on the condition of women in nineteenth-century England. It is, to be honest, a rather tedious paragraph, but Miss Brontë manages a tactful balance in it between the obvious truth of Caroline's complaints and the ironic juxtaposition of her musings to the active lives of Shirley and Miss Ainsley, women too busy for such reveries or for worrying about injustice to themselves:

'The brothers of these girls are every one in business or in professions; they have something to do: their sisters have no earthly employment, but household work and sewing; no earthly pleasure, but an unprofitable visiting; and no hope, in all their life to come, of anything better. . . . The great wish—the sole aim of every one of them is to be married, but the majority will never marry: they will die as they now live. They scheme, they plot, they dress to ensnare husbands. The gentlemen turn them into ridicule: they don't want them; they hold them very cheap: they say—I have heard them say it with sneering laughs many a time—the matrimonial market is overstocked. Fathers say so likewise, and are angry with their daughters when they observe their manœuvres: they order them to stay at home. What do they expect them to do at home? If you ask,—they would answer, sew and cook. They expect them to do this, and this only contentedly, regularly, uncomplainingly all their lives long, as if they had no germs of faculties for anything else: a doctrine as reasonable to hold, as it would be that the fathers have no faculties but for eating what their daughters cook, or for wearing what they sew. Could men live so themselves? Would they not be very weary? . . . Men of England! look at your poor girls, many of them fading round you, dropping off in consumption or decline; or, what is worse, degenerating to sour old maids,

—envious, backbiting, wretched, because life is a desert to them: or, what is worst of all, reduced to strive, by scarce modest coquetry and debasing artifice, to gain that position and consideration by marriage which to celibacy is denied. Fathers! cannot you alter these things? . . . Keep your girls' minds narrow and fettered—they will still be a plague and a care, sometimes a disgrace to you: cultivate them—give them scope and work—they will be your gayest companions in health; your tenderest nurses in sickness; your most faithful prop in age.' [Chap. 22, ii:271–4.] The words are put in Caroline's mouth, but the sentiments are clearly Miss Brontë's; elsewhere there is little evidence that Caroline is capable of such extended thought, and in any case there is no one more anxious to be simply mate, mother, and house-keeper.

The difference between Caroline's conventional views of woman's place and Shirley's vision of her sex as exalted creatures of infinite capability, comes out most clearly in the scene after the school-feast, when the two girls descend the hill to the church, which Shirley cannot bear to enter be-cause of its heat and the dreary, conventional orations she knows the clergy will be making. Caroline is nervous at missing the service, but Shirley has her own pantheistic devotions to make: 'Nature is now at her evening prayers: she is kneeling before those red hills. . . . Caroline, I see her! and I will tell you what she is like: she is like what Eve was when she and Adam stood alone on earth.'

Caroline suggests that the vision is unlike Milton's Eve. 'Milton's Eve!' Shirley exclaims: 'Milton's Eve! I repeat. No, by the pure Mother of God, she is not! . . . Milton tried to see the first woman; but, Cary, he saw her not. . . . It was his cook that he saw; or it was Mrs. Gill, as I have seen her, making custards in the heat of summer, in the cool dairy. . . . I would beg to remind him that the first men of the earth were Titans, and that Eve was their mother: from her sprang Saturn, Hyperion, Oceanus; she bore Prometheus— . . . I saw—I now see—a woman-Titan: her robe of blue air spreads to the outskirts of the heath. . . . So kneeling, face to face she speaks with God. That Eve is Jehovah's daughter, as Adam was His son.'

Caroline retreats into religious and social orthodoxy and objects that this Eve is pagan. 'She is very vague and visionary! Come, Shirley, we ought to go into church.' Shirley, in the grip of a larger perception, refuses: 'Caroline, I will not: I will stay out here with my mother Eve, in these days called Nature.'

Hardly at home in such empyrean flights, Caroline seizes upon what she understands, to return her thoughts to the comfort for which she so longs. The word 'mother' suggests to her 'imagination not the mighty and mystical parent of Shirley's visions, but a gentle human form—the form she ascribed to her own mother; unknown, unloved, but not unlonged-for. "Oh, that the day would come when she would remember her child! Oh, that I might know her, and knowing, love her!" Such was her aspiration.'[1] [Chap. 18, II:163–6.]

As the two girls turn towards home, they meet the misogynist Joe Scott, who voices what are essentially Caroline's opinions, although she hates hearing them put into words, even those of St. Paul: 'Let the woman learn in silence, with all subjection. I suffer not a woman to teach, nor to usurp authority over the man; but to be in silence. For Adam was first formed, then Eve. . . . Adam was not deceived; but the woman, being deceived, was in the transgression.' [Chap. 18, II:176.]

The theme of the titan-woman is continued in Louis's recitation of Shirley's juvenile composition, in which she tells of

[1] It is probably significant that Caroline is the only character in the novel who longs for the comfort of a mother, although all the other major characters are actually orphans, if that word is applicable to adults. It is a curious fact that in Miss Brontë's novels all the central figures except Caroline are parentless; of the secondary characters only Dr. John and Polly in *Villette* have even one parent living.

the first woman, 'Eva', and her union (described in highly sexual terms) with the Comforter: the bridal-hour of Humanity and Genius. Caroline's idea of paradise is a domestic one, the cottage at the mill; 'the little parlour of that house was her earthly paradise; how she longed to return to it, as much almost as the First Woman, in her exile, must have longed to revisit Eden.' [Chap. 13, ii:61.]

Shirley is always Caroline's leader; she climbs walls, jumps hedges, restraining Caroline's emotions during the siege of the mill and preventing her from rushing headlong among the fighting to be with Robert and, as Shirley points out, to be nothing but a nuisance to him. Without a second thought she orders bedding, clothing, and wine to be sent from Fieldhead to the wounded soldiers and rioters, while Mrs. Pryor wonders impotently whether it would be proper to do so. We are meant to see the likeness in the hesitancy of Mrs. Pryor and in the nervousness with which Caroline approaches even so simple a matter as ordering a meal for visitors in her own house.

The stoic courage with which Shirley faces suffering is indicated by her description of the sterilization of the dog bite that she receives: 'While the maid was busy crimping or starching, I took an Italian iron from the fire, and applied the light scarlet glowing tip to my arm: I bored it well in: it cauterized the little wound. Then I went up-stairs.' [Chap. 28, iii:130.] It is like a literal remembrance of the narrator's metaphorical advice on how to act when fate puts the scorpion of pain into one's palm: 'Show no consternation: close your fingers firmly upon the gift; let it sting through your palm. Never mind: in time, after your hand and arm have swelled and quivered long with torture, the squeezed scorpion will die, and you will have learned the great lesson how to endure without a sob.' The advice is given in reference to Caroline, but it is Shirley who exemplifies it.

Yet all this is not to suggest that Shirley is meant as an ideal, Caroline someone to be despised. Each has qualities the other lacks. If Shirley has courage, dignity, and pride, Caroline has boundless sympathy with those she loves. Feminine traits are as necessary in the world as the masculine, and either can become dangerous if they exclude the other. Caroline, by the end of the book, has learned partially to control her emotions, and she has learned, through the cruel encounter with Mrs. Yorke, to defend her own attitudes. Shirley has learned to love as an equal and to share her responsibilities. Were they to remain as they were at the beginning of the book, there would be danger of Caroline's developing into the shrinking woman that her mother is, afraid of life and love, constantly worried about the respectability and conventionality of actions. Mrs. Yorke, on the other hand, stands as a warning to Shirley, the mature woman into which she might grow without the civilizing influences of love: hard, haughty, proud, scornful of beauty and sparse of affection.

The spectre of spinsterhood that haunted Miss Brontë is personalized in the vignettes of Miss Mann and Miss Ainsley, the old maids of the story, reacting in opposite ways to the loneliness of their lives. Miss Mann becomes increasingly withdrawn and censorious, aware of the lack of respect that society feels for her, and resentful of it, brave but afraid to show her bravery: the objectification of Caroline's fears for her own life. Hortense Moore, too, shows how the spinster becomes totally uninterested in anything but 'correct' learning and an obsessive cleanliness around the house. As if to indicate that circumstances need not dictate personality, Miss Brontë includes the portrait of Miss Ainsley, serene, benign, charitable; her life, according to Mr. Hall, 'came nearer the life of Christ, than that of any other human being he had ever met with'. [Chap. 10, 1:268.] It is, however, an austere conception of life that only a Christian hero could hope to undertake in happiness.

As in the other novels, there is a vast range of choice, and Caroline and Shirley must tread a tight-rope in finding their places in the world. Spinsterhood is unattractive, but clearly marriage fails for many. Mr. Helstone is too hard to make a success of his marriage, Mrs. Pryor too soft to succeed in holding together a marriage to a selfish man, and both believe that the institution itself is little more than a purgatory. Some men like Yorke marry while they are still in love with other women, and can see only monetary advantages in the marriages of others. The ideal that Miss Brontë holds out is a high one, and it is not surprising that some readers feel that Caroline gets worse than she deserves in marrying Robert, whose vision of the future is less of a home than of a model community with a mill that he runs, while Caroline looks after the feminine side of the settlement: 'The copse shall be firewood ere five years elapse: the beautiful wild ravine shall be a smooth descent; the green natural terrace shall be a paved street: there shall be cottages in the dark ravine, and cottages on the lonely slopes: the rough pebbled track shall be an even, firm, broad, black, sooty road, bedded with the cinders from my mill: and my mill, Caroline—my mill shall fill its present yard.' The houseless, starving, and unemployed, he tells Caroline 'shall come to Hollow's Mill from far and near; and Joe Scott shall give them work, and Louis Moore, Esq. shall let them a tenement, and Mrs. Gill shall mete them a portion till the first pay-day.' The reader is reminded of the ending of *Major Barbara*, with its vision of a neat factory town, full of contented workers, whose souls are handed over to the distaff side. 'Such a Sunday-school as you will have, Cary! such collections as you will get! such a day-school as you and Shirley, and Miss Ainsley, will have to manage between you! The mill shall find salaries for a master and mistress, and the Squire or the Clothier shall give a treat once a quarter.' [Chap. 37, III:314–15.] If this is heaven, the heart scarcely leaps at it. Man and woman, husband and wife, remain separate in function and sympathies, no longer grown into one flesh, one soul. Nowhere does the novel seem more sober, more disillusioned than in the conventional 'happy' ending.

The much abused historical background of the novel is not the irrelevancy for which it is sometimes taken. It is true that Miss Brontë's imagination was less stirred by the social and political panorama--even that of Yorkshire--than by the turmoil of private emotion or the drama of the conflicting tugs of conscience, but we know from Mrs. Gaskell how intently the entire Brontë family, from childhood onward, followed the newspapers and their accounts of domestic and international political events. In this novel that part of man's interests that the Victorians thought of as a specifically masculine preserve becomes a projection of the harder side of the rational aspect of the mind and personality. The political and economic concerns of the men operate in *Shirley* in much the same way that St. John's pietistic disregard of the emotions works in *Jane Eyre*: they are misguided because one-sided. Caroline lacks self-reliance because she is too emotional; the men become hard and uncharitable through too little emotional empathy with others.

In this novel Miss Brontë is deliberately broadening her canvas, but in so doing she reverses the usual process of the social novel of her day. In the works of Dickens, George Eliot, Kingsley, or even Thackeray and Trollope, the lives and actions of the characters serve as microcosmic examples of what is ailing England and the world. In *Shirley* the Luddite riots, the Orders in Council, the opposing interests of Tory and Whig are employed to throw light on the intensely personal conflicts that lie at the core of the novel, acting almost as metaphors to extend the significance of those conflicts. The horizons are broader, but the focus of attention remains as confined as ever it was in *Jane Eyre* or *The Professor*. The concentration of the novel remains steadfastly on the individual not the nation, and we should be thankful that Miss Brontë realized that her talents were not for the full-scale social novel; the Romantic muse is not always at ease when her attention shifts from the particular to the general.

The growth of the Industrial Revolution, with its breaking of many of the old social links, is background to the disintegration of personal relationships. 'National honour was become a mere empty name of no value in the eyes of many, because their sight was dim with famine, and for a morsel of meat they would have sold their birthright.' [Chap. 2, 1:38.] There are no outright villains in the book except the organizers of the discontent among the workmen, but most of the men in the novel in their own ways set class against class, interest against interest, while undertaking their actions in the name of justice. Helstone, the extreme Tory, wants only justice for the propertied classes, and if that means hardship for the employed, so much the worse for them. The stern defender of rank and privilege, he is haughty to his associates, whom he secretly despises, and believes that the cures for the general unrest are 'vigorous government interference, strict magisterial vigilance; when necessary, prompt military coercion.' [Chap. 4, 1:74.] So absolute is his sense of divine hierarchy that he confuses disrespect to the king with blasphemy to God.

Yorke, the representative of the established manufacturing classes, hates all centralized authority with a kind of reverse snobbishness, since he is 'without the organ of Veneration'. [Chap. 4, 1:62.] He and Helstone quarrel constantly on the subject, but they are equally guilty of snobbery, whether straightforward or inverted. Yorke's relations with his social inferiors are excellent because 'they, while submitting implicitly to his influence, never acknowledged, because they never reflected on, his superiority; they were quite tractable, therefore, without running the smallest danger of being servile; and their unthinking, easy, artless sensibility was as acceptable, because as convenient, to Mr. Yorke, as that of the chair he sat on, or of the floor he trod.' [Chap. 4, 1:68.]

The Coriolanian Robert Moore, as a foreigner and outsider, has no fixed social or political or patriotic principles save an unhesitating allegiance to what will benefit himself.

He is benevolent to well-disposed workmen, but he never considers the possibility of their rights having any claim on him; he is contemptuous of their abilities and motives, and considers an informed charity to be possible only when the manufacturer is completely secure from reprisal. He sticks at Helstone's sermons on the divine right of kings while insisting on his own divine right to do as he pleases. Miss Brontë probably intended him to be in part a representative of the Manchester school of economics and philosophy, as yet unawakened to his human responsibilities, like Carlyle's Plugson of Undershot. If Helstone and Yorke err through class prejudice, Moore errs through cold-hearted, thoroughly rational self-consideration, and the result is that there is little to choose between the three men.

Of the employers in the novel, only Shirley Keeldar combines charity towards her economic inferiors with so strong a sense of her own position and aristocracy as to preclude snobbery. She is brusque with the ignorant or unfeeling when they attempt to threaten her or to act as her equals, but she has no hint of condescension towards anyone who is truly not her inferior in any way but birth and fortune. She represents the older aristocratic position, one slowly being overtaken by the Moores and Yorkes. Half woman, half man, she occupies the intermediate position between the feminine world of intuition and emotion and the masculine world of reason, where the softer feelings have no place.

That Miss Brontë 'got up' her material from the files of the Leeds newspapers for the facts of the Luddite risings has been taken as evidence of her inadequacy for writing a social novel; the fact is without significance, for what she was writing was not a social novel at all, but a study of private emotion and thought in which the conflict is not primarily between master and man, Tory and Whig, but between the feminine viewpoint and the essentially masculine outlook of the world of commerce and politics. Unlike her other novels. *Shirley* contains no real resolution of the problem. The marriage of

Robert and Caroline is not the final union of two persons who have learned much and found a single outlook inadequate; it is the mating of totally different persons who will presumably remain unlike forever. In Miss Brontë's favourite word, they do not suit. Between them, they cover much of the spectrum of human possibility, but as individuals, or even as mates, they remain incomplete. Louis and Shirley come closer to Miss Brontë's ideal of the union of lovers who are almost identical in their outlooks, but they are not greatly changed from what they were, and their eventual marriage is the result of having triumphed over external difficulties only. There is little of the feeling that man's nature is refined through struggle, love is no longer the metaphorical reward for growth, and the result is a novel of lessened stature.

The Victorian age was one of spaciousness in the novel; the mandatory three volumes not only fostered it, it demanded world enough and time, and Miss Brontë usually developed her themes and characters with the air of being unhampered by such considerations as brevity. *Shirley* is a long novel, indeed, but the ending is curiously huddled and cramped. This effect is no doubt due in part to there being, as has been suggested, no real resolution; the strings of the puppets are jerked, they pair off, and the stage is cleared. The effect has its most unfortunate result in the character of Louis Moore, who is introduced late in the book. Clearly, he is intended as a model for the other characters in the novel, but like Shirley he is not given an opportunity to exercise his own character, and he remains passive throughout almost all the action in which he is concerned.

Louis Moore is learned, and we are told (although it is not demonstrated) that he becomes a model squire of Fieldhead, carrying on and amplifying the traditions of Shirley herself. Besides his masculine attributes—which, significantly, do not include good looks[1]—he is quiet and has an almost

---

[1] Like Rochester, who is said to resemble his dog Pilot, he is told by Shirley that he looks like her mastiff Tartar.

feminine gentleness. 'I see now it is Hortense, Louis resembles, not Robert,' [Chap. 23, ii:305.] Caroline says on first meeting him. When Mrs. Sympson leaves Fieldhead, Louis writes in his notebook: 'I have long since earned her mother's undying gratitude by my devotion to her boy: in some of Henry's ailments I have nursed him—better, she said, than any woman could nurse: she will never forget that.' [Chap. 36, iii:292.] He has the depth of emotion that is needed to complement his masculinity, just as Shirley has the independence of mind and spirit denied such womanly women as Caroline, and the combination of qualities is obviously the synthesis that Miss Brontë is advocating in the novel. Unfortunately, she is never able to bring Louis to life.

With Robert she is more convincing because she never attempts to open his heart to the reader; his handsome exterior, so baffling to both Caroline and Shirley, is presented successfully because he is usually seen from their viewpoint. Miss Brontë felt compelled to disclose Louis's gentler side, and to do so, she had to resort to the artistically crude method of having him confide his most intimate thoughts to his notebook. She could portray the façade of rough masculinity, but the mind of a gently virile man eluded her, and the result is that his scribbling sounds too much like that of a genteel young girl. The device of his secret notebook is doubly disappointing because his retelling of the major scenes between himself and Shirley denies them the dramatic vitality that they might have had in direct narration.[1]

'And after all, authors' heroines are almost as good as authoress's heroes,' Caroline assures Shirley, who replies with her usual spirit: 'Not at all: women read men more

[1] The same objection might be made to Robert's account of his rejection by Shirley, although here the method is almost redeemed by the description of her reaction to his proposal: 'Instead of faltering a sweet Yes, or maintaining a soft, confused silence (which would have been as good) she started up, walked twice fast through the room, in the way that *she* only does, and no other woman, and ejaculated,—"God bless me!" ' [Chap. 30, ii:163–4.] Suddenly, we no longer feel the filter of Moore's personality between us and the events he describes.

truly than men read women.' [Chap. 20, II:210.] The male
reader can only beg to demur.

In many ways *Shirley* is Miss Brontë's most ambitious
novel, but it is a long way from being her most successful.
The reason for her failure is not, I think, the generally
accepted one that she knew too little of social history to deal
with the situation of 1812, but rather that she attempted to
split her sensibility in too many directions, divided it among
too many characters, tried to encompass too many viewpoints, and to see them all objectively. She was no Jane
Austen, capable of detachment, nor was she a George Eliot,
able to give full emotional validity to several points of view;
the result is a series of fragments, many of them splendid.
Fortunately, in her last completed novel she returned to the
single point of view that had worked so well in *Jane Eyre*.

4

VILLETTE

In the generosity of her feeling for Mrs. Gaskell, Miss Brontë insisted that *Villette* should not be published until her friend's current novel was already on the market and in the hands of the reviewers, so that her own work should not 'come in the way of *Ruth*'. *Villette*, she wrote to Mrs. Gaskell, 'has indeed no right to push itself before *Ruth*. There is a goodness, a philanthropic purpose, a social use in the latter, to which the former cannot for an instant pretend; nor can it claim precedence on the ground of surpassing power: I think it much quieter than *Jane Eyre*.' [Gaskell, Chap. 26, II:277.] A quiet book her last novel is, indeed: autumnal, full of resignation and acceptance, and probably the culmination of her brief artistic career. Retrospect, we must remember, too often tempts us into seeing a conclusion in what is merely the final work of an artist's life. Beethoven's last quartets, *The Tempest*, Verdi's *Falstaff*, Yeats's late poems: it is seductive to feel that these represent the peaks towards which their creators struggled, forgetting that range after range might have come into their view had time or circumstance not cut off their artistic lives. And so it is with Charlotte Brontë: the basic optimism of *The Professor* and *Jane Eyre* is followed by the bleakness of *Shirley*. As synthesis follows thesis and antithesis, *Villette* takes cognizance of both sorrow and joy, and integrates them into a grave, tragic, awareness of the mixed lot and nature of man and accepts them with neither gladness nor rancour but a serenity that has no precedent in her work. What might have succeeded had Miss Brontë not died in her thirty-ninth year, we can hardly guess (certainly, the fragment of a novel called *Emma* is no indication), but *Villette* remains as the capstone to her artistic life.

In *Villette* there is a full awareness that human justice is fallible, and that even divine favour is partial, but where in *Shirley* there is a sense of religion as providing no comfort in this world, *Villette* is unobtrusively full of hints that Miss Brontë had accepted the traditional view of human redemption as not only transcending earthly life but also throwing over it the comforting awareness that human sorrow is at worst transient. 'I suppose, Lucy Snowe,' the narrator tells herself, 'the orb of your life is not to be so rounded; for you the crescent-phase must suffice. Very good. I see a huge mass of my fellow-creatures in no better circumstances. I see that a great many men, and more women, hold their span of life on conditions of denial and privation. I find no reason why I should be of the few favoured. I believe in some blending of hope and sunshine sweetening the worst lots. I believe that this life is not all; neither the beginning nor the end. I believe while I tremble; I trust while I weep.' [Chap. 31; III:78–9.]

Rather than appearing oblivious of the suffering of man, as *Shirley* seems to suggest, God plans for His creatures in this book in ways too mysterious for human comprehension. When Lucy foretells the future for Polly, she speaks, if not in Miss Brontë's own voice, at least in harmony with the tenor of the whole novel: 'Some lives *are* thus blessed: it is God's will: it is the attesting trace and lingering evidence of Eden. Other lives run from the first another course. Other travellers encounter weather fitful and gusty, wild and variable—breast adverse winds, are belated and overtaken by the early closing winter night. Neither can this happen without the sanction of God; and I know that, amidst His boundless works, is somewhere stored the secret of this last fate's justice: I know that His treasures contain the proof as the promise of its mercy.' [Chap. 32, III:110–11.] In *Villette* there is still an awareness of the suffering in store for most men, but it no longer seems purposeless; the difference in attitudes is vast.

In the act of accepting the necessity for suffering lies its balm. In *Villette* Miss Brontë has stopped protesting against the injustice of a Christian fate that she can neither control nor understand, and the result is a distinct lessening of the dissatisfaction and agony that suffuses *Shirley*. The calm acceptance of the inequalities of life is an indication of her double view that man's duty is to strive towards perfection at the very moment that he is only too conscious that earthly reward is never consistent with that endeavour, and that conventional happiness cannot be counted on as fair wages for honest striving. It is a tragic view of life, but as in all true tragedy, knowledge and awareness are themselves an amelioration of pain, and the consequent dignity of the individual triumphs over any inclination to self-pity and makes the pity of others unimportant. Tragic awareness precludes the acceptance of happiness exacted at the cost of easy, inferior, or ignoble aims.

This is the only one of Miss Brontë's novels that does not conclude with what is at least a conventionally happy ending to the plot. The progression in the endings of the four novels is interesting. In *The Professor* Crimsworth and Frances marry happily, have a son, and gain sufficient material comforts. There is no important impediment to their attainment of happiness; only the recognition of mutual love and the resolve to work hard are necessary for the fulfilment of life. The course of the narrative is direct, almost linear. In *Jane Eyre* there is the first awareness that temporal happiness is not the normal lot of man, that it is not to be expected, or to be gained without payment. By the end of the novel the marriage of Jane and Rochester becomes the reward for passionate striving towards perfection, achieved only after the pain of burning out the ignoble aspects of one's nature. The greater the potentiality of that nature, the greater the final happiness, but also the greater the pain of achieving it

In *Shirley* marriage, wealth, and social position are doled out to Shirley, Caroline, and the Moore brothers, but they have become gifts not rewards, and they seem almost derisory, for they no longer stand metaphorically for any moral perfection of the characters. *Villette* suggests that for a few fortunates of the world, moral goodness and temporal happiness may exist together, but for the majority of mankind there is no necessary correlation between those qualities. The children of fortune, like Polly and Dr. John, sail serenely past the shoals of the world, perhaps drawing little water but never hitting the rocks. The Ginevras and the de Hamals of the world exist on a lower moral plane but never come to grief. Even the morally reprehensible of the world meet no temporal retribution. The last words of the novel are both born of a painfully achieved tolerance and coloured with irony: 'Madame Beck prospered all the days of her life; so did Père Silas; Madame Walravens fulfilled her ninetieth year before she died. Farewell.' [Chap. 42, iii:350.]

Yet this is not to suggest that *Villette* sets forth the world as a moral anarchy, nor does it suggest ultimate injustice for man. To be sure, Lucy and Paul never marry, and their one moment of complete unity is agonizingly brief. Untouched by the smile of fortune, they are the world's inhabitants who must continue to strive even while they accept that temporal rewards are not to be theirs. To perceive happiness is as much as we can expect; if human aspiration is sincere, earthly reward for it is finally unimportant. Few would wish to repay Lear for his suffering by restoring him to his throne. It may, indeed, be true that when she wrote this novel, Miss Brontë had come to accept her perpetual severance from M. Héger and had reasoned herself into believing that the existence of her love was more important than its fulfilment; whatever the biographical circumstances, surely what matters to us is that she wrote in *Villette* a story of suffering and renunciation with meaning far beyond her own experiences in an obscure Brussels *pension*.

Human injustice in this novel is the parallel in actuality to what cosmic injustice appears to be at first sight. Almost all the characters in the book are unfair to the motivations of others, and Lucy herself finds that one of the most difficult attributes of maturity to acquire is that of justice to others. From her initial misjudgment of Polly to her hallucinatory tour of the fête, where she constantly misjudges the other major characters of the novel, she is premature, unfair, and illogical in her assessment of others. Even while she is learning justice herself, she is aware of its rarity in human relations, and when she is asked by the examiners to write on the subject of 'Human Justice', she portrays her as 'a red, random beldame', smoking a pipe and drinking whisky: 'she smoked and she sipped and she enjoyed her paradise, and whenever a cry of the suffering souls about her pierced her ears too keenly—my jolly dame seized the poker or the hearth-brush: if the offender was weak, wronged, and sickly, she effectually settled him; if he was strong, lively, and violent, she only menaced, then plunged her hand in her deep pouch, and flung a liberal shower of sugar-plums.' [Chap. 35, III:162–3.]

As has been suggested, *Shirley* is far from a conventionally Christian novel, with its increased emphasis on a humanistic creed and morals, with man making his own fate as he lives among the dead forms of Christianity. In *Villette* there is a resurgence of Christian faith, but with great importance still accorded to individual choice and judgment, in short, to what Miss Brontë thought of as the Protestant strain of Christianity. Lucy goes 'by turns, and indiscriminately' to the Presbyterian, Lutheran, and Episcopalian chapels of Villette. 'Now, it happened that I had often secretly wondered at the minute and unimportant character of the differences between these three sects—at the unity and identity of their vital doctrines: I saw nothing to hinder them from being one day fused into one grand Holy Alliance, and I respected them all, though I thought that in each there were faults of form;

incumbrances, and trivialities. Just what I thought, that did I tell M. Emanuel, and explained to him that my own last appeal, the guide to which I looked, and the teacher which I owned, must always be the Bible itself, rather than any sect, of whatever name or nation.' [Chap. 36, III:196.] In this novel, for the first time, Miss Brontë uses her anti-Roman Catholic emotions thematically and adequately as she equates Roman doctrines and practices with emotionalism as excesses of the undisciplined aspect of man's nature, the submission of reason and will to the irrational.

Christian faith and endurance are so embedded into this novel that it is difficult to abstract passages to illustrate Miss Brontë's thesis without relying on the more conventional exhortations of the text. At the beginning of the chapter called 'Cloud', after telling of the future happiness of Polly and Dr. John, Lucy reflects upon her own state: 'His will be done, as done it surely will be, whether we humble ourselves to resignation or not. The impulse of creation forwards it; the strength of powers, seen and unseen, has its fulfilment in charge. Proof of a life to come must be given. In fire and in blood, if needful, must that proof be written. In fire and in blood do we trace the record throughout nature. In fire and in blood does it cross our own experience. Sufferer, faint not through terror of this burning evidence. Tired wayfarer, gird up thy loins; look upward, march onward. Pilgrims and brother mourners, join in friendly company. Dark through the wilderness of this world stretches the way for most of us: equal and steady be our tread; be our cross our banner. For staff we have His promise, whose "word is tried, whose way perfect": for present hope His providence, "who gives the shield of salvation, whose gentleness makes great"; for final home His bosom, who "dwells in the height of Heaven"; for crowning prize a glory, exceeding and eternal. Let us so run that we may obtain; let us endure hardness as good soldiers; let us finish our course, and keep the faith, reliant in the issue to come off more than conquerors: "Art thou not from ever-

lasting mine Holy One? WE SHALL NOT DIE!" ' [Chap. 38,
III:234–5.] The style is perilously close to cant, but its ur-
gency is evidence of the thematic importance to Miss
Brontë of the passage.

Miss Brontë's growth as a novelist is nowhere more
evident than in her use of the point of view from which
Villette is told. As she had done twice before, she wrote the
entire novel with the main character as narrator, but Lucy
Snowe is her first whole-hearted attempt at the use of an
'unreliable narrator'. In *The Professor* she aimed at objectivity in spite of the first-person narration, and almost as if to
allow herself but scant identification with the narrator, she
told the story through the mouth of Crimsworth. Although
he is hardly a success as a masculine character, he does serve
to increase the detachment—with nearly disastrous results.
Jane Eyre as a narrator swings to the opposite end of the
scale, since her adult perceptions and attitudes can, with a
few exceptions, be taken as the point of view of the author
herself; the identification is almost complete. *Shirley*, as we
have seen, is an attempt to combine the factual quality of a
detached narrator with the immediacy provided by a sensibility divided between Caroline and Shirley.

Miss Brontë's frequently expressed feelings of dislike for
Lucy Snowe, the narrator and central figure of *Villette*, are
adequate indicators that the viewpoints of the narrator and
of the author are not intended to be taken as coincident.[1]
Throughout the novel we are expected as readers to evaluate
Lucy's perceptions constantly, for they are partial or mistaken as often as not. Miss Brontë first gave her the name
under which she appears in the novel, then changed it to
'Frost' before reconsidering the change and restoring the
original name. 'A *cold* name she must have,' Miss Brontë

[1] It is only fair, however, to note that the intention of the author cannot
always be identified with her accomplishment. Polly, for instance, is subtly but
definitely disparaged as one of that lesser breed, fortune's darlings, although
Miss Brontë told George Smith that she intended her as 'the most beautiful'
character in the book. [Gaskell, Chap. 25, II:272.]

told Williams: 'partly, perhaps, on the *"lucus a non lucendo"* principle—partly on that of the "fitness of things", for she has about her an external coldness.' [Gaskell, Chap 25, II:267.] On another occasion she told Smith that 'I am not leniently disposed towards Miss *Frost*: from the beginning, I never meant to appoint her lines in pleasant places.' [Gaskell, Chap. 25, II:265.] Lucy's inadequacies (indeed, her whole character) are less attractive than those of Jane Eyre, and we judge them more harshly, as Miss Brontë clearly intended. By the end of the novel Lucy has outgrown most of her narrow views and uncharitable modes of action, but until that point we are expected to make constant comparison between her behaviour and that we might hope for in a more generous, clear-sighted character.

Miss Brontë in *Villette* is once more occupied with the problem of the relationship between the rational and the non-rational faculties. Lucy, like Jane Eyre, is torn between these conflicting claims, but unlike Jane she is not initially attracted by the warmth of passion or dismayed at the chilliness of its lack. As a girl she is almost without sympathy for others and incapable of love, having none of the generous spirit that so often nearly causes Jane to go too far towards the dangers of passion.

In the early scenes at Bretton Lucy is initially disdainful of affection, and it is only long after Polly has arrived there with her father that Lucy feels the first slow stirrings of the unawakened, or stifled, feelings of compassion that lie hidden in the depths of her personality. When she first sees Polly kneeling in her bed, 'praying like some Catholic or Methodist enthusiast—some precocious fanatic or untimely saint', for her father, Lucy's unsympathetic reaction is that Polly is 'betraying that monomaniac tendency I have ever thought the most unfortunate with which man or woman can be cursed'. 'These sudden, dangerous natures—*sensitive* as they are called—offer many a curious spectacle to those whom a cooler temperament has secured from participation in their angular

VILLETTE

151

vagaries.' [Chap. 2, 1:16–17.] Polly's reunion with her father 'was not a noisy, not a wordy scene: for that I was thankful; but it was a scene of feeling too brimful, and which, because the cup did not foam up high or furiously overflow, only oppressed one the more. On all occasions of vehement, unrestrained expansion, a sense of disdain or ridicule comes to the weary spectator's relief. . . .' [Chap. 2, 1:19.] When Polly helps with her father's tea, Lucy's reaction once more is censorious: 'Candidly speaking, I thought her a little busy-body; but her father, blind like other parents, seemed per-fectly content to let her wait on him, and even wonderfully soothed by her offices.' [Chap. 2, 1:22.] When her father leaves once more, Polly calls his name in misery: 'During an ensuing space of some minutes, I perceived she endured agony. . . . Nobody spoke. Mrs. Bretton, being a mother, shed a tear or two. Graham, who was writing, lifted up his eyes and gazed at her. I, Lucy Snowe, was calm.' [Chap. 3, 1:34–5.] Self-possession has seldom seemed more damning.

During the absence of her father, Polly's infantile affec-tions naturally turn to John,[1] 'a handsome, faithless-looking youth of sixteen . . . A spoiled, whimsical boy.' [Chap. 2, 1:23–4.] Because she is unable to understand affection or the need for it, Lucy is inclined towards 'improving the occasion by inculcating some of those maxims of philosophy whereof I had ever a tolerable stock for application'. With a good sense she seldom displays, Polly rebels: 'She stopped me, however, by putting her fingers in her ears at the first words I uttered, and then lying down on the mat with her face against the flags.' [Chap. 3, 1:43–4.]

That Lucy has the germ of a heart is indicated in Polly's last night at Bretton when Lucy carries her to John for a last goodnight and then invites her to get into bed with her, 'wishing, yet scarcely hoping, that she would comply: for

[1] Since young Bretton's change of Christian name from Graham to John is confusing in discussion, it is simplest to call him by the name he is known by during most of the book.

she was a most strange, capricious little creature, and especially whimsical with me. She came, however, instantly, like a small ghost gliding over the carpet. I took her in. She was chill; I warmed her in my arms. She trembled nervously; I soothed her. Thus tranquillized and cherished she at last slumbered.' [Chap. 3, 1: 59.]

This first section of the novel is one which has frequently baffled readers who fail to see that its primary function is to establish Lucy's character, not those of Polly and John, and who therefore feel that Miss Brontë's focus changes during the course of the story. Actually, of course, the characters of Polly and John are being established as well, but what is reported of them is not meant to be swallowed whole. Our natural reaction as readers is to demand black and white, to feel that what we learn of these two important persons must be either completely trustworthy or wholly false, but Miss Brontë is attempting something more difficult, the establishment of a certain triviality in Polly and John at the same time that Lucy's inadequate sympathies are condemned in her own words.

That Lucy is something of a prig is adequately shown at Bretton, but the hints of the bigger nature beneath really await their development until she goes to live with Miss Marchmont as her unwilling companion. At the level of foreshadowing, Miss Marchmont stands as a portent of Lucy's future life, both in the loss of her own lover and in the decency and honesty that inform her superficially unattractive character.[1] More importantly, however, Miss Marchmont provides Lucy with the opportunity to see how wrong her own first impressions can be and how easy it is for her to be unjust. 'Closer acquaintance, while it developed both faults and eccentricities, opened, at the same time, a view of a character I could respect. Stern and even morose as she

[1] Lucy's presentiment at the sound of the spring wind serves to foretell Miss Marchmont's death, and it also establishes the mood of prescience and foreshadowing that makes credible the relevance of Miss Marchmont's life to Lucy's future.

sometimes was, I could wait on her and sit beside her with that calm which always blesses us when we are sensible that our manners, presence, contact, please and soothe the persons we serve.' [Chap. 4, 1:66.] Miss Marchmont's religious sense also stands as a model for that which Lucy comes to accept by the end of the novel: 'We should acknowledge God merciful, but not always for us comprehensible. We should accept our own lot whatever it be, and try to render happy that of others.' [Chap. 4, 1:75.]

After Miss Marchmont's death, Lucy is cheated by an avaricious heir of the inheritance she has been promised (although his avarice later relents, at least to the limit of one hundred pounds), but what she has learned from the old woman is worth more than the money Lucy expects: 'a vein of reason ever ran through her passion; she was logical even when fierce'. [Chap. 4, 1:66.]

Since Miss Marchmont serves as the first model for Lucy, it may reasonably be objected that Miss Brontë fails to make her character either interesting enough or developed at sufficient length to sustain the thematic importance intended for it. Certainly, the spinsters of *Shirley*, her counterparts in that novel, are far more memorable; Miss Marchmont cannot be counted among Miss Brontë's successes.

The death of her mentor makes Lucy, like Jane at Lowood, anxious to leave the circumscribed life she has hitherto led and to try her wings in larger surroundings: 'Who but a coward would pass his whole life in hamlets, and for ever abandon his faculties to the eating rust of obscurity?' The moment has come for her to change from the observer of life to a participant. 'I had a sudden feeling as if I, who never yet truly lived, were at last about to taste life: in that morning my soul grew as fast as Jonah's gourd.' [Chap. 6, 1:86.] In the life at Bretton she had been superior to Polly's inexperience; in London and Villette she becomes totally naïve herself, tricked by porters, victimized by watermen, and patronized by waiters.

The brief scene of Lucy's nocturnal boarding of the ship *Vivid* for Boue-Marine is one of the most striking in the book, as she journeys into the unknown. 'Down the sable flood we glided; I thought of the Styx, and of Charon rowing some solitary soul to the Land of Shades.' [Chap, 6, 1:92.] Ironically, her trip is not to the land of the dead, as she fears, but to life itself. It is, however, a kind of life that she is as yet unequipped to understand, for it will involve her in the dark turmoil of the emotions.[1] 'I asked myself if I was wretched or terrified. I was neither. Often in my life have I been far more so under comparatively safe circumstances. "How is this?" said I. "Methinks I am animated and alert, instead of being depressed and apprehensive?" I could not tell how it was.' [Chap. 6, 1:92.]

With Lucy's involvement in life, the problem of justice and kindness to others broadens out into the question of the identity of other human beings, who they are, and how one is to know them, as well as how to treat them. Inevitably, this poses for Lucy the more important problem of self-knowledge, of finding out her own identity. The attempt to discover who she is becomes in part an attempt to find out for herself how much allegiance she owes to the reason, how much to passion and imagination. These two parallel problems of identity and of the importance of rationality occupy the rest of the book, crossing and recrossing, occasionally fusing into a joint question, so that it is difficult to untwine the two threads and examine them separately.

As an Englishwoman of good social standing (we are told that her station is the same as that of the Brettons), correct demeanour, cold Anglo-Saxon rationality, and strict Protestant views, Lucy naturally despises everything that is Labassecourien. Her attitude is indicated by the names in this fictional version of Belgium. 'Labassecour' means farmyard,

[1] How deeply Charlotte Brontë felt her own departure for Brussels was an expedition into the mysterious is indicated by her letter to her sister Emily (see p. 161).

'Boue-Marine' is ocean-mud, and 'Villette', the 'great capital of the great kingdom of Labassecour', actually means a small city.[1] Initially, she sees only ignorance, slothfulness, greed, and corruption in the inhabitants of her new home; it takes three volumes to teach her the partiality of her views.

As a result, in part, of her insular prejudices, Lucy discovers the strength of her own passion as she falls in love with Dr. John Bretton, whose surname suggests both his nationality and his quality. He is taller than the Labasse-couriens, fair (red-haired, to tell the truth), 'a true young Englishman', who 'might be a lord, for anything I knew: nature had made him good enough for a prince'. As Lucy follows him through the park, she reflects that she would follow 'that frank tread, through continual night, to the world's end'. [Chap. 7, I:117, 118.] Later in the book Mrs. Bretton asks whether her son has 'not rather the air of an incipient John Bull? He used to be slender as an eel, and now I fancy in him a sort of heavy-dragoon bent—a beef-eater tendency.' [Chap. 17, II:45.] Lucy is to discover the limitations of England, as she finds virtues in Villette.

Lucy's mounting experience of passion, the imagination, illusion, and the rest of the non-rational faculties are developed in a series of big scenes, almost set-pieces, reminiscent in their self-contained, theatrical quality of the 'Eden' scene in *Jane Eyre*. The culmination of this group of scenes takes place at the midnight fête at the end of the book, but the recurrent background to them is the *allée défendue* in the school garden, suggesting by its name both the prohibition against its use and the forbidden love of the nun said to have been entombed there alive at the foot of Methusaleh, the ancient pear tree. The sense of venturing into forbidden realms frequently colours what occurs in the secluded walk.

Miss Brontë makes complicated use of the figure of the nun as it appears from time to time in the novel. On the first

[1] For still further examples, see Georgia S. Dunbar, 'Proper Names in *Villette*', *Nineteenth-Century Fiction*, vol. 15, no. 1, June 1960, pp. 77–80.

level it is, of course, a reminiscence of the Gothic novel, and the appearance of the veiled figure is used straightforwardly for a heightening of the emotional tension of the moment, to give the true Gothic *frisson*. But at the same time Miss Brontë is deliberately inverting the Gothic tradition by showing that the nun is actually only a silly young man disguised in order to gain access to a girls' school. The lurid imagination of the Gothic tradition is thus set against the rational explanation, in the mode that Prof. Robert B. Heilman has called the 'anti-Gothic'.[1] So far the juxtaposition of points of view is not far from that of comedy, where common sense reigns triumphant and pierces to the truth behind illusion. This is the method of *Northanger Abbey* or even of *Cold Comfort Farm*. But Miss Brontë's purpose is not comic. For her, common sense alone is insufficient, and imagination need not be illusion; she is concerned with the truth of *both* the view of common sense and that of the imagination. Since she can no longer expect readers to take the literal appearance of the nun as credible by anything but a diseased fancy, she gives psychological validity to its nocturnal wanderings by making them coincide with those moments when Lucy is most distraught emotionally. As readers we know there must be a pedestrian explanation for the figure, but we still get the old *frisson*: not because the manifestation is inexplicable but because it is completely understandable as an objective correlative for Lucy's emotions. The effect is directly comparable to the psychological truth of the haunting of Thornfield by Bertha Rochester. If Jane Austen was one remove from the Gothic tradition in inverting it, Miss Brontë is two removes from it, re-inverting the old counters and giving them new meaning.

The initial recounting of the nun's legend occurs long before the first appearance of the figure, but its introduction into the story is coincident with the first pangs of passion that

[1] See his essay on 'Charlotte Brontë's "New Gothic",' probably the most brilliant essay yet written about her works.

Lucy feels. As she walks through the garden, under a crescent moon, thinking of the legend, the box of violets and its accompanying note are thrown into the *allée*. In the subsequent conversation with John, Lucy feels the stirrings of love. When Lucy sees Mme. Beck searching her belongings for the note, she first laughs and then cries. 'I never had felt so strange and contradictory an inward tumult as I felt for an hour that evening: soreness and laughter, and fire, and grief, shared my heart between them. I cried hot tears; not because Madame mistrusted me—I did not care twopence for her mistrust—but for other reasons. Complicated, disquieting thoughts broke up the whole repose of my nature.' [Chap. 13, 1:232.] The unsettling mixture of feelings that overwhelm her indicate the profoundly disrupting quality of the advent of passion in her life.

The next of the big scenes in which Lucy's emotional development is displayed is the play given on the night of Mme. Beck's fête. When she is asked to take a leading part at short notice, Lucy finds 'a thousand objections. . . . The foreign language, the limited time, the public display. . . .' [Chap. 14, 1:262.] But M. Paul, who sees the necessity for Lucy to enlarge the scope of her emotional life, insists that she take part in the drama: 'I will not have you shrink, or frown, or make the prude. I read your skull, that night you came; I see your moyens: play you can; play you must.' [Chap. 14, 1:260.] Her unwillingness to assume a full man's costume in the play is one of the more ambiguous aspects of the episode. She dresses for the part as a man from the waist upward but wears her dun-coloured skirt rather than breeches. 'M. Paul might storm, might rage: I would keep my own dress.' [Chap. 14, 1:271.] Miss Brontë clearly intended more by Lucy's strange manner of dressing than a display of mere conventional modesty. The probable psychological explanation (in terms of the content of the novel, not the psychiatrist's couch) involves Lucy's continued resistance to M. Paul's dominant insistence on involving her in the drama.

Reluctantly she is allowing herself to become partially engaged with a world of emotion outside her former cool role
as observer. 'A keen relish for dramatic expression had revealed itself as part of my nature; to cherish and exercise
this new-found faculty might gift me with a world of delight,
but it would not do for a mere looker-on at life.' [Chap. 14,
1:277.] That this is the intent of the scene is made more
credible by a comparison with the other primarily theatrical
scene in the novel, that of the performance of Vashti. Further-
more, since Vashti's abandon in her part is one of emotion, of
sexual passion (which shocks Lucy), it seems reasonable that
Lucy's reserve in play-acting indicates her own fear of the
same sort of abandon in herself.[1]

On the night when the violets and note land at her feet,
Lucy confesses to a hyper-sensitivity to the weather which
'woke the being I was always lulling, and stirred up a craving
cry I could not satisfy'. [Chap. 12, 1:211.] This elemental
surging of emotion is what Miss Brontë meant by hypochondria, with its implications of the abandonment of reason.
The hypochondriac manifestations return in the chapter
called 'The Long Vacation'. The change of weather intensi-
fies the loneliness of Lucy, living in the empty school with
only the cook and an imbecile pupil: 'I do not know why that

[1] I repeat that the 'psychological' sense of which I write is only an attempt
to see what Miss Brontë was accomplishing in novelistic technique, not what a
Freudian psychologist or psychiatrist might discover there. The latter might,
however, be interested in the frequency with which Miss Brontë describes male
characters in female terms, and in the fact that Rochester, Lucy, de Hamal, and
Dr. John all assume the clothing of the opposite sex. Miss Brontë wrote to
Ellen Nussey in 1843: 'I admire exceedingly the costume you have chosen to
appear in at the Birstall rout. I think you say pink petticoat, black jacket, and a
wreath of roses—beautiful! For a change I would advise a black coat—velvet
stock and waistcoat—white pantaloons and smart boots!' [SHB, 1:285.] Some
three years earlier she had written to Wordsworth, in connection with whether
her sex had any relevance to her artistic ambitions: 'Several young gentlemen
curl their hair and wear corsets, and several young ladies are excellent whips
and by no means despicable jockeys.' [SHB, 1;212.] The narrator of her first
novel is a man, and she fought to keep the masculine anonymity of her pen-
name, Currer Bell. Shirley Keeldar, of course, constantly refers to herself in
masculine terms. What significance, if any, there is in all this is probably a
matter for the biographer not the critic.

change in the atmosphere made a cruel impression on me, why the raging storm and beating rain crushed me with a deadlier paralysis than I had experienced while the air had remained serene; but so it was; and my nervous system could hardly support what it had for many days and nights to undergo in that huge, empty house.' [Chap. 15, 1:310.] The direction her longing is taking is indicated by her irrational envy of Ginevra for being loved, although in calmer moments she has a faint contempt for her: 'One day, perceiving this growing illusion, I said, "I really believe my nerves are getting overstretched: my mind has suffered somewhat too much; a malady is growing upon it—what shall I do? How shall I keep well?" ' [Chap. 15, 1:314.] The bitterness of loneliness comes to her metaphorically in a draught that prefigures the drug she swallows on the night of the carnival, when she is to escape into the city on a long walk seeking relief, as she does on this occasion: 'Between twelve and one that night a cup was forced to my lips, black, strong, strange, drawn from no well, but filled up seething from a bottomless and boundless sea. Suffering, brewed in temporal or calculable measure, and mixed for mortal lips, tastes not as this suffering tasted.' [Chap. 15, 1:315.] When the cook urges her to call a doctor, she refuses, saying, 'I thought no doctor could cure me.' [Chap. 15, 1:316.] The irony may be unconscious, but it is effective in its reference to Dr. John.

When, in the agony of her hypochondria, Lucy makes her strange, Protestant confession to Père Silas, she has reached what is for her the abyss of total abandonment of will, giving over her soul to another in the fashion she so dislikes in Roman Catholics. The incident, like so many others in the book, is drawn directly from Miss Brontë's own experiences in Brussels. In September 1843, she wrote an account of her own confession to her sister Emily, which indicates the importance she attached to the act of a Protestant seeking Roman relief:

'More than half the holidays are now past, and rather

better than I expected. The weather has been exceedingly
fine during the last fortnight, and yet not so Asiatically hot
as it was last year at this time. Consequently I have tramped
about a great deal and tried to get a clearer acquaintance
with the streets of Bruxelles. This week, as no teacher is
here except Mdlle. Blanche, who is returned from Paris, I
am always alone except at meal-times, for Mdlle. Blanche's
character is so false and so contemptible I can't force myself to
associate with her. She perceives my utter dislike and never
now speaks to me–a great relief.

'However, I should inevitably fall into the gulf of low
spirits if I stayed always by myself here without a human being to speak to, so I go out and traverse the Boulevards and
streets of Bruxelles sometimes for hours together. Yesterday
I went on a pilgrimage to the cemetery, and far beyond it on
to a hill where there was nothing but fields as far as the
horizon. When I came back it was evening; but I had such a
repugnance to return to the house, which contained nothing
that I cared for, I still kept threading the streets in the
neighbourhood of the Rue d'Isabelle and avoiding it. I found
myself opposite to Ste. Gudule, and the bell, whose voice you
know, began to toll for evening *salut*. I went in, quite alone
(which procedure you will say is not much like me), wan-
dered about the aisles where a few old women were saying
their prayers, till vespers begun [*sic*]. I stayed till they were
over. Still I could not leave the church or force myself to go
home–to school I mean. An odd whim came into my head.
In a solitary part of the Cathedral six or seven people still
remained kneeling by the confessionals. In two confessionals
I saw a priest. I felt as if I did not care what I did, provided
it was not absolutely wrong, and that it served to vary my
life and yield a moment's interest. I took a fancy to change
myself into a Catholic and go and make a real confession to
see what it was like. Knowing me as you do, you will think
this odd, but when people are by themselves they have singular fancies. A penitent was occupied in confessing. They do

not go into the sort of pew or cloister which the priest occupies, but kneel down on the steps and confess through a
grating. Both the confessor and the penitent whisper very
low, you can hardly hear their voices. After I had watched
two or three penitents go and return, I approached at last and
knelt down in a niche which was just vacated. I had to kneel
there ten minutes waiting, for on the other side was another
penitent invisible to me. At last that went away and a little
wooden door inside the grating opened, and I saw the priest
leaning his ear towards me. I was obliged to begin, and yet
I did not know a word of the formula with which they always
commence their confessions. It was a funny position. I felt
precisely as I did when alone on the Thames at midnight. I
commenced with saying I was a foreigner and had been
brought up a Protestant. The priest asked if I was a Protestant then. I somehow could not tell a lie, and said "yes". He
replied that in that case I could not *"jouir du bonheur de la
confesse"*; but I was determined to confess, and at last he said
he would allow me because it might be the first step towards
returning to the true church. I actually did confess—a real
confession. When I had done he told me his address, and
said that every morning I was to go to the rue du Parc—to
his house—and he would reason with me and try to convince
me of the error and enormity of being a Protestant!!! I
promised faithfully to go. Of course, however, the adventure
stops there, and I hope I shall never see the priest again. I
think you had better not tell papa of this. He will not understand that it was only a freak, and will perhaps think I am
going to turn Catholic.' [Shorter, 1:270–71.]

'It was no impetus of healthy feeling which urged her to
the confessional,' Miss Brontë wrote of Lucy to Williams;
'. . . it was the semi-delirium of solitary grief and sickness.'
[Gaskell, Chap 25, 11:268.] The mental distress that drives
her to confession is also responsible for her misinterpretation
of Père Silas, who, as she suspects, would gladly make a con-
vert of her but who is also the agent of saving her and getting

her to the ministrations of Dr. John. Priest and doctor aid her
in soul and body, but she is able to recognize kindliness only
in the physician of the flesh, for she is as apt to erroneous
prejudice about institutions as she is about persons. It is the
first indication in the novel or, for that matter, in any of
Miss Brontë's novels that Roman Catholicism may have
virtues in spite of being unattractive to her. The point is important because of the final acceptance in the novel of M.
Paul's religion as part of the life of a good man.

Her convalescence at La Terrasse, miles outside Villette, is
Lucy's symbolic retreat to her English childhood and to a
lack of involvement with the greater world. Surrounded by
English friends and the household gods of her youth, she
gives over her will to John and Mrs. Bretton, just as she has
attempted to do with Père Silas. But emotion has grown in
the ten years separating her from the house at Bretton. Her
love for John she 'entreated Reason betimes to check. . . .
"let me be content with a temperate draught of this living
stream".' [Chap. 16, II:28.] Miss Brontë does not over-
emphasize the point, but Lucy has become, in fact, as child-
ishly infatuated with John as Polly was at Bretton; the setting
and action are the same, the characters different.

The theme of the danger of unleashed passions is carried
forward in the episode in the picture gallery, which is as near
as Miss Brontë comes in this novel to an extended humorous
scene. The depth of Lucy's emotion has frightened her away
from full participation in the play, and it has swept her into
the confessional, but the pictorial representation of sensuality
fails to move her, just as Polly's emotion had failed to move
her at Bretton, since it is no longer obviously connected with
her own psyche. With heavy jocularity she muses on the
Cleopatra of the picture, who weighs 'from fourteen to sixteen stone. She was, indeed, extremely well fed: very much
butcher's meat—to say nothing of bread, vegetables, and
liquids—must she have consumed to attain that breadth and
height, that wealth of muscle, that affluence of flesh. She lay

half-reclined on a couch: why, it would be difficult to say; broad daylight blazed round her; she appeared in hearty health, strong enough to do the work of two plain cooks; she could not plead a weak spine; she ought to have been standing, or at least sitting bolt upright. She had no business to lounge away the noon on a sofa. She ought likewise to have worn decent garments; a gown covering her properly, which was not the case: out of abundance of material—seven-and-twenty yards, I should say, of drapery—she managed to make inefficient raiment.'[1] [Chap. 19, II:71.]

Lucy's humorous contempt for the Cleopatra tells us a good deal about her own lack of knowledge that she has anything in common with 'this huge, dark-complexioned gipsy-queen', but Miss Brontë also uses the picture as a touchstone for three other important characters. Colonel de Hamal with his pretty head, a 'highly polished little pate', his 'trim and natty' figure, 'womanish feet and hands', is 'exceedingly taken' with the painting and titters and whispers to a friend about the charms of the 'dusk and portly Venus'. [Chap. 19, II: 81–2.]

Opposed to de Hamal's salacious fascination with the figure is the lack of interest shown by Dr. John: 'he did not

---

[1] This is one place in the novel where the critic would like to know more about Miss Brontë's life in order to understand her technique more fully. I have been unable to find the 'original' of the Cleopatra, if, indeed, Miss Brontë had one particular picture in mind. To compare it to Lucy's description might tell us a good deal about Miss Brontë's method of using autobiography in her novels, since we should then have a concrete, visual object with which to compare the literary creation. The description of the figure sounds as if it were a Rubens painting, and later Lucy compares Vashti to the Cleopatra, to the disadvantage of the painting, and suggests that Vashti would disperse Rubens and 'all the army of his fat women', but I have been unable to find that Rubens painted a Cleopatra. The surrounding vases, goblets, draperies, jewels, and flowers are not unlike the backgrounds of some Pre-Raphaelite paintings, however, and the tone of the passage is so scornful that it would seem likely that Miss Brontë had in mind more immediate, contemporary painters, rather than one so long dead as Rubens. It may be that she was combining memories of the many Rubens paintings in Brussels with details from more modern paintings that she had seen in her several London trips in the year or two before writing *Villette*, for there she visited both public and private galleries, and there she saw Rachel, whose acting inspired the Vashti episode.

simper like the little Count; his mouth looked fastidious, his eye cool. . . .' On leaving the gallery he says to Lucy: 'I heard some French fops, yonder, designating her as "le type du voluptueux"; if so, I can only say, "le voluptueux" is little to my liking.' [Chap. 19, II:83–4.]

Halfway between de Hamal's coarseness and Dr. John's cold, detached view of the flagrantly physical is the attitude of M. Paul, who finds the Cleopatra disturbing but immoral. Of all those who look at the picture, only he takes it entirely seriously: 'Une femme superbe—une taille d'impératrice, des formes de Junon, mais une personne dont je ne voudrais ni pour femme, ni pour fille, ni pour sœur.' [Chap. 19, II:80.] Paul's penetrating understanding of Lucy's nature dates from the night of their first meeting at Mme. Beck's, when he read her physiognomy and answered Mme. Beck's question as to whether the face betrayed good or bad qualities: 'Of each kind, without doubt.' [Chap. 7, I:125.] On the night of the play he recognized her need to assume a fuller role in life; at the picture gallery he recognizes the dangers for her of undisciplined passion. To her irritation, he suggests that she study, instead of the Cleopatra, the four panels depicting woman's life as young girl, bride, young mother, and widow. 'All these four "Anges" were grim and gray as burglars, and cold and vapid as ghosts.' [Chap. 19, II:75–6.] So long as she sees no relevance to herself, Lucy can continue her detached, superior view of passion, unaware of its danger. Only on her attendance at the performance of Vashti does she recognize its perils.

Between the episode in the gallery and the Vashti scene intervenes another set-piece, the concert, as well as the first two visitations of the nun, which make Lucy's reactions to the actress quite different from her view of the painting. The concert scene advances the plot by showing John's growing distaste for Ginevra, and it serves as a foil to the Vashti scene, since in both cases Lucy is a member of the audience, but with totally different reactions. At the concert Lucy for the first time wears gala evening dress, her initial commitment to the world of fashion and, like Ginevra's finery, a gift from wealthier friends. She tempers its pink splendour with a black mantel, but its effect is still so unlike her usual severity as to anger M. Paul when he sees it, and significantly she fails to recognize herself when she passes before a great mirror. The vapid, pleasure-seeking aspect of the world she is seeing for the first time is typified by the silly behaviour of Ginevra and her companion, Lady Sara. 'You look,' says M. Paul when he meets Lucy after the concert, 'like one who would snatch at a draught of sweet poison, and spurn wholesome bitters with disgust.' [Chap. 21, ii:137.] His dislike of what he persists in calling her 'scarlet' gown is partially motivated by jealousy of John, but beyond that he perceives the impropriety of Lucy's entering the world that the dress represents.

There is a verbal echo of Paul's words when Lucy receives her first letter from John:[1] 'Of course, happiness of such shallow origin could but be brief; yet, while it lasted, it was genuine and exquisite: a bubble—but a sweet bubble—of real honey-dew.' [Chap. 22, ii: 162-3.] The honey-dew proves sweet poison. Lucy's behaviour at receiving the letter is precisely like the later actions of Polly on receiving her own letter from John. Each examines the envelope, the writing, and marvels over the vermilion seal before daring to open it. The rising excitement that Lucy feels is given objective expression by the appearance of the nun as she reads the letter in the attic of the school. She totally loses her reason at the loss of the letter, crawling on the floor, wringing her hands, betraying all the excess of emotion that she has despised.[2]

[1] The infrequency of John's letters and the emotional turmoil that they arouse in Lucy are set in direct contrast to the letters that she receives from Paul: 'By every vessel he wrote; he wrote as he gave and as he loved, in full-handed, full-hearted plenitude. . . . his letters were real food that nourished, living water that refreshed.' [Chap. 42, iii:346-7.]

[2] Lucy now applies the word to herself with which she has damned Polly at Bretton: ' "Oh! they have taken my letter!" cried the grovelling, groping *monomaniac*.' [Chap. 22, ii:166; italics mine.] The comparison can hardly be

The danger of overemotion into which Lucy has fallen is indicated when she writes answers to John's letters: 'To begin with: Feeling and I turned Reason out of doors, drew against her bar and bolt, then we sat down, spread our paper, dipped in the ink an eager pen, and, with deep enjoyment, poured out our sincere heart.' 'Reason' makes her substitute cooler replies. 'She did right.' [Chap. 23, ii:180–82.]

Almost as if recounting the history of a fever, Miss Brontë speeds up the succession of big scenes as she approaches the Vashti episode, the hectic climax of Lucy's unhealthy feeling of her passions for John. The nun reappears as Lucy is dressing for the theatre, preparing her for the emotion she is to experience that evening.

We know how deeply shaken Miss Brontë had been by the experience of seeing Rachel perform, from the series of letters she wrote, almost compulsively, about the great actress. Over and over she equated Rachel's art with a hellish yielding to passion, and it is this aspect that she portrays so forcefully in writing of Vashti in the novel. To Ellen Nussey she wrote of Rachel: 'a wonderful sight–terrible as if the earth had cracked deep at your feet, and revealed a glimpse of hell. I shall never forget it. She made me shudder to the marrow of my bones; in her some fiend has certainly taken up an incarnate home. She is not a woman; she is a snake; she is the–' [Gaskell, Chap. 23, ii:216.] Rachel was, she told Sydney Dobell, 'I know not what, I think a demon. I saw her in Adrienne Lecouvreur and in Camilla–in the last character I shall *never* forget her–she will come to me in sleepless nights again and yet again. Fiends can hate, scorn, rave, wreathe [writhe?], and *agonize* as she does, not mere men and women. I neither love, esteem, nor admire this strange

---

accidental, for she longs successively for John and Paul, just as Polly has grieved over her father's absence and John's; before going to confession, she kneels in bed in hypochondriacal prayer, as Polly has done at Bretton; and in the conclusion of the book she serves Paul ('With what shy joy I accepted my part as hostess, arranged the salver, served the benefactor-guest!') as Polly has served tea to her father and John.

being, but (if I could bear the high mental stimulus so long),
I would go every night for three months to watch and study
its manifestations.' [*SHB*, III: 253.] And to James Taylor
she wrote months later, as if unable to exorcize the memory:
'Rachel's acting transfixed me with wonder, enchained me
with interest, and thrilled me with horror. The tremendous
force with which she expresses the very worst passions in
their strongest essence forms an exhibition as exciting as the
bull-fights of Spain and the gladiatorial combats of old Rome,
and (it seemed to me) not one whit more moral than these
poisoned stimulants to popular ferocity.' [Shorter, II:252.]

The long Vashti episode is probably the most powerful of
all Miss Brontë's extended descriptive writing, evoking
literally the sense of presence at great but frightening theatrical ritual, and symbolically the splendour and horror of
unleashed passion.

'She rose at nine that December night: above the horizon I
saw her come. She could shine yet with pale grandeur and
steady might; but that star verged already on its judgment-
day. Seen near, it was a chaos—hollow, half-consumed: an orb
perished or perishing—half lava, half glow. . . . Behold! I
found upon her something neither of woman nor of man: in
each of her eyes sat a devil. . . . They wrote HELL on her
straight, haughty brow. They tuned her voice to the note of
torment. They writhed her regal face to a demoniac mask.
Hate and Murder and Madness incarnate she stood.

'It was a marvellous sight: a mighty revelation.

'It was a spectacle low, horrible, immoral. . . .

'Scarcely a substance herself, she grapples to conflict with
abstractions. Before calamity she is a tigress; she rends her
woes, shivers them in convulsed abhorrence. . . . Fallen,
insurgent, banished, she remembers the heaven where she
rebelled. Heaven's light, following her exile, pierces its confines, and discloses their forlorn remoteness.

'Place now the Cleopatra, or any other slug, before her as
an obstacle, and see her cut through the pulpy mass as the

scimitar of Saladin clove the down cushion.' [Chap. 23,
II: 188–91.]

This time there is no need for the presence of M. Paul to
point out to Lucy the danger of what she is seeing, but when,
as she has done at the gallery, she turns to John to see his
reaction, she finds him unmoved. 'His natural attitude was
not the meditative, nor his natural mood the sentimental;
impressionable he was as dimpling water, but, almost as water,
unimpressible. . . . Dr. John *could* think, and think well, but
he was rather a man of action than of thought; he *could* feel,
and feel vividly in his way, but his heart had no chord for
enthusiasm. . . . When I took time and regained inclination
to glance at him, it amused and enlightened me to discover
that he was watching that sinister and sovereign Vashti, not
with wonder, nor worship, nor yet dismay, but simply with
intense curiosity. Her agony did not pain him, her wild
moan—worse than a shriek—did not much move him. . . .
"How did he like Vashti?" I wished to know.

' "Hm-m-m," was the first scarce articulate but expressive
answer; and then such a strange smile went wandering round
his lips, a smile so critical, so almost callous!' [Chap. 23,
II: 192–4.]

Lucy has frequently before noticed John's shortcomings,
and she has even denied to herself that she loves him, but it is
the combination of the depth of her own emotion at the play
and the sight of John's unfeeling face that finally helps her to
recover from her fever for him. As John has been cured by
Ginevra's behaviour at the concert, so here at the play his
own manner effects the restoration of Lucy's emotional
equilibrium. Full health is slow in coming, but the danger
is past.

'Towards midnight, when the deepening tragedy blackened to the death scene, and all held their breath, and even
Graham bit in his under lip, and knit his brow, and sat still
and struck—when the whole theatre was hushed, when the
vision of all eyes centred in one point, when all ears listened

towards one quarter—nothing being seen but the white
form sunk on a seat, quivering in conflict with her last, her
worst-hated, her visibly-conquering foe—nothing heard but
her throes, her gaspings, breathing yet of mutiny, panting
still defiance: when, as it seemed, an inordinate will, con-
vulsing a perishing mortal frame, bent it to battle with doom
and death, fought every inch of ground, sold every drop of
blood, resisted to the latest the rape of every faculty, *would*
see, *would* hear, *would* breathe, *would* live, up to, within,
well nigh *beyond* the moment when death says to all sense
and all being—

 ' "Thus far and no farther!" ' [Chap. 23, ii:194–5.]

When the stretching of the emotions is no longer tolerable,
fire breaks out in the theatre like a metaphorical repetition of
the purging holocaust of Thornfield. That the flame is only a
loose hanging quickly quenched is irrelevant; the way is clear
for John to turn to his natural mate, Polly, and for Lucy to
turn to Paul.

It would be a falsification of both plot and theme in the
novel to suggest that Lucy's love for John follows a linear
course up to the Vashti episode, and that then she switches
direction and heads equally directly towards the final love
scene with M. Paul in the Faubourg Clotilde. The novel
simply is not that schematic, and there are several indications
that Lucy finds John dangerously attractive throughout her
life, even if the feeling she has for him operates at a much less
mature level than her love for Paul. She tells Polly bluntly
that she seldom looks at John's masculine beauty because 'I
value vision, and dread being struck stone blind'. [Chap. 37,
iii:208.] At the carnival she reflects upon her place in his
affections: 'I kept a place for him, too—a place of which I
never took the measure, either by rule or compass: I think it
was like the tent of Peri-Banou. All my life long I carried it
folded in the hollow of my hand—yet, released from that hold
and constriction, I know not but its innate capacity for expanse might have magnified it into a tabernacle for a host.'

[Chap. 38, iii:274–5.] The difference between Lucy's feelings
for John and the more temperate feelings of the second half
of the novel is indicated by Paul's outburst when he thinks
that Lucy has refused to take notice of his birthday: 'False
and cold, I don't think you are; but you have made a great
mistake in life, that I believe: I think your judgment is
warped–that you are indifferent where you ought to be
grateful–and perhaps devoted and infatuated, where you
ought to be cool as your name. Don't suppose that I wish you
to have a passion for me, Mademoiselle; Dieu vous en garde!
What do you start for? Because I said passion? Well, I say it
again. There is such a word, and there is such a thing–
though not within these walls, thank Heaven! You are no
child that one should not speak of what exists; but I only
uttered the word–the thing, I assure you, is alien to my
whole life and views. It died in the past–in the present it lies
buried–its grave is deep-dug, well-heaped, and many win-
ters old.' [Chap. 29, iii:45–6.]

Probably in no other Victorian novel is there such an adult
recognition that a woman's sexual attraction to one man may
persist beyond the growth of love for another. Mature love
may succeed mere physical excitement, but it need not
destroy it. Small wonder that Miss Brontë's contemporaries
found her novels dangerously outspoken.

In the second half of the novel, as Lucy learns a new kind
of love, the method of exposition becomes less theatrical. The
'big scenes' of the school play, the confessional, the gallery,
the concert, and Vashti's performance have all been cast in
terms of the artificiality of the theatre or art (the frequent
references to the theatricality of the Roman Catholic church
are sufficient evidence that Miss Brontë saw much of it in
terms of play-acting). In the latter half of the book there are
but two repetitions of this kind of scene, the visit to Mme. Walravens and the long night of hallucination at the carnival.

Before these two scenes, however, come the last two visitations of the nun. The first of these occurs when Lucy is

burying her letters from John (and her hopes for a future
with him) at the foot of Methusaleh, where the body of the
original nun and her forbidden feelings are interred. (The
likeness between Lucy's symbolic act and Paul's reference
to the grave of his earlier passion is obvious.) The nun's last
visit occurs when Paul has told Lucy implicitly that he loves
her, by saying that they are born under the same star and
that their destinies are intertwined. Both visitations come at
moments of heightened emotion, but the second time Lucy
sees the apparition in company with Paul, who feels as she
does, apprehensive but unafraid, aware that whatever the
nun may represent is something that they share. Affection
and reason may rob even the supernatural of its terror,
passion of its dangers.

Lucy must, however, undergo the visit to Mme. Walravens
alone, and she is not yet ready to evaluate that frightening
household accurately. The house becomes the objectification
of all that she fears in Roman Catholicism and in that primitive layer of the personality where reason does not penetrate.
As the other emotionally heightened scenes have been
couched in the language of theatre and artifice, this is saturated with the sense of superstition. The aged crone lives in
'old and grim Basse-Ville' under the shadow of 'the venerable
and formerly opulent shrine of the Magi', with its three half-
ruined towers celebrating the 'three mystic sages of a dead
and dark art'; in the ancient house the inhabitants speak 'the
aboriginal tongue of Labassecour'. The barbarically dressed
old woman is 'Cunegonde, the sorceress! Malevola, the evil
fairy'. At her turning, 'a peal of thunder broke, and a flash of
lightning blazed broad over salon and boudoir. The tale of
magic seemed to proceed with due accompaniment of the
elements. The wanderer, decoyed into the enchanted castle,
heard rising, outside, the spell-wakened tempest.' [Chap. 34,
III: 137.] The priest of this strange shrine to the past is Père
Silas, representative of what Lucy both longs for and dreads
in the confessional, and in place of the nun in the garden is the

portrait of Justine Marie in conventual robes. 'I thought of the apparition when I saw the portrait,' [Chap. 35, III:174] Lucy tells Paul.

There is nothing to fear in the house of the old hunchback save what Lucy brings herself, the willingness to fear, just as there has been nothing intrinsically dangerous in the apparition of the nun of the *berceau*. Painfully she has learned that the appearance of persons need not indicate their inner qualities; a red beard, Grecian profile, and a tall, erect carriage[1] need not mean a warm and magnanimous nature in an English doctor who looks like a prince, and a shapeless nose, unbrushed clothes, and sallow complexion do not make M. Paul despicable. She has yet to learn that Paul may serve Mme. Walravens, even be a Roman Catholic Labassecourien, and still retain the integrity and independence of his own soul. The lessons of the reason are painful.

The last of the great theatrical scenes in the book takes place in the midnight park; it is told in flashes, with all the surrealistic clarity of a nightmare, as the fragments of Lucy's experience tumble forth in a chain of association, linking all the major characters of the book and tying together the images and themes of the theatre, the picture gallery, the Roman Catholic Church, Labassecour, the ancient Basse-Ville, and the other sinister associations of what Lucy thinks of as the Imagination.

The opiate that Goton administers to Lucy stimulates her rather than lulling her mind: 'Instead of stupor, came excitement. I became alive to new thought–to reverie peculiar in colouring. A gathering call ran among the faculties, their bugles sang, their trumpets rang an untimely summons. Imagination was roused from her rest, and she came forth impetuous and venturous. With scorn she looked on Matter, her mate–

[1] Both Dr. John's physical description and his name inevitably recall those of St. John Rivers in *Jane Eyre*; in both cases physical beauty covers a real inadequacy of character.

' "Rise!" she said. "Sluggard! this night I will have *my* will; nor shalt thou prevail." ' [Chap. 38, III:258–9.]

In the park the characters are real, taking part in a commonplace provincial fête, but to Lucy's fancy their significance is mysterious, and under the influence of the drug her imagination turns the placid family groups into cabals from whose mysteries she is banned. With the fancy released from the inhibitions of the reason, her subconscious tumbles forth fragmentary hints of the scenes of the past connected with her unfettered feelings; although her love has changed from John to Paul, the imagination feeds on the same symbols. Timber, paint, and pasteboard combine in a giant theatrical set to create 'a land of enchantment, a garden most gorgeous, a plain sprinkled with coloured meteors, a forest with sparks of purple and ruby and golden fire gemming the foliage; a region, not of trees and shadow, but of strangest architectural wealth—of altar and of temple, of pyramid, obelisk, and sphinx; incredible to say, the wonders and the symbols of Egypt teemed throughout the park of Villette.' [Chap. 38, III:264–5.] In the Egyptian symbols, there is perhaps a hint of her memory of the Cleopatra of the picture gallery, and the obsessive experience of the confessional returns in the vision 'of altar and of temple'. 'On this whole scene was impressed a dream-like character; every shape was wavering, every movement floating, every voice echo-like—half-mocking, half-uncertain.' [Chap. 38, III:266.]

The mood of theatricality that has suffused the earlier scenes returns, and each group of persons becomes the cast of characters in a drama whose meaning escapes Lucy: 'Somehow I felt, too, that the night's drama was but begun, that the prologue was scarce spoken: throughout this woody and turfy theatre reigned a shadow of mystery; actors and incidents unlooked-for, waited behind the scenes; I thought so: foreboding told me as much.' [Chap. 38, III:275.] Like supernumeraries in a theatrical spectacle, the crowd drifts by, masked and costumed.

The English miss is caught up in a night of Labasse-courien national glory, the little Protestant walks among the 'troops of priests in the park that night'. Like a vignette from La Terrasse, her English friends sit placidly, with John looking enquiringly at her disguise, but when Lucy moves away from them to come upon the foreign 'junta', the group is dominated by the wicked winking of Mme. Walravens's jewels and the Popish habit of Père Silas. All the major characters of the book are assembled in Lucy's waking nightmare, and among them she moves, disguised, unrecognized, the dreamer of the dream.

As the name of Justine Marie has pierced Lucy in the Rue des Mages, so now it brings to a head her misery when it is pronounced. 'Hint, allusion, comment, went round the circle, but all so broken, so dependent on references to persons not named, or circumstances not defined, that, listen as intently as I would—and I *did* listen *now* with a fated interest—I could make out no more than that some scheme was on foot, in which this ghostly Justine Marie—dead or alive—was concerned.' [Chap. 39, III:286.]

The apparition of the nun has previously accompanied the wash of emotion; now the mention of the nun of the Rue des Mages sets the undisciplined imagination running wild: 'I called up to memory the pictured nun on the panel; present to my mind was the sad love-story; I saw in thought the vision of the garret, the apparition of the alley, the strange birth of the berceau: I underwent a presentiment of discovery, a strong conviction of coming disclosure. Ah! when imagination once runs riot where do we stop? What winter tree so bare and branchless—what wayside, hedge-munching animal so humble, that Fancy, a passing cloud, and a struggling moonbeam, will not clothe it in spirituality, and make of it a phantom?' [Chap. 39, III:286–7.]

Fancy, whose other name tonight is jealousy, has always distorted Lucy's vision, and tonight it makes her see the young Justine Marie as Paul's beloved, not the mere ward that she is, and it causes her to believe that Paul has joined the junta against her. But Fancy has in store for Lucy the last and most cruel illusion, the belief that Fancy itself is a hard-won vision of the truth, to whose temple she has finally penetrated: 'Thus it must be. The revelation was indeed come. Presentiment had not been mistaken in her impulse: there is a kind of presentiment which never *is* mistaken; it was I who had for a moment miscalculated; not seeing the true bearing of the oracle, I had thought she muttered of vision when, in truth, her prediction touched reality.

'I might have paused longer upon what I saw; I might have deliberated ere I drew inferences. Some, perhaps, would have held the premises doubtful, the proofs insufficient; some slow sceptics would have incredulously examined, ere they conclusively accepted the project of a marriage between a poor and unselfish man of forty, and his wealthy ward of eighteen; but far from me such shifts and palliatives, far from me such temporary evasion of the actual, such coward fleeing from the dread, the swift-footed, the all-overtaking Fact, such feeble suspense of submission to her the sole sovereign, such paltering and faltering resistance to the Power whose errand is to march conquering and to conquer, such traitor defection from the TRUTH. . . .

'In my infatuation, I said, "Truth, you are a good mistress to your faithful servants! While a Lie pressed me, how I suffered! Even when the Falsehood was still sweet, still flattering to the fancy, and warm to the feelings, it wasted me with hourly torment. The persuasion that affection was won could not be divorced from the dread that, by another turn of the wheel, it might be lost. Truth stripped away False-hood, and Flattery, and Expectancy, and here I stand—free!"' [Chap. 39, III:293-5.]

When she returns to the sleeping school, Lucy is convinced that at last she has conquered the weakness of imagination and love, and she is determined to root such infirmities out of her life. She tries to rid herself of what she thinks of as

hysteria by destroying the dummy nun lying on her bed, unaware that her thoughts and actions are hysterical in themselves. 'Tempered by late incidents, my nerves disdained
hysteria. Warm from illuminations, and music, and throng-
ing thousands, thoroughly lashed up by a new scourge, I
defied spectra. In a moment, without exclamation, I had
rushed on the haunted couch . . . I tore her up—the incubus!
I held her on high—the goblin! I shook her loose—the mystery! And down she fell—down all round me—down in shreds
and fragments—and I trod upon her.'[1] [Chap. 39, III:300.]

At the moment Lucy accepts her action as a final victory of
reason and the routing of all emotion, but we as readers know
that her perceptions are faulty because they are still clouded
by the heady drug of fancy. To her the rending of the nun's
habit stands for the complete rooting out of love, but we,
recognizing that throughout the book the appearances of the
nun have been associated with overemotionalism, know that
what is being destroyed is only the diseased excess of emotionalism, and that the way is being prepared for a mature
reconciliation with Paul, based on reasonable love and whole-
hearted rationality. Only the discarded clothes of an unhealthy theatricality have been torn to fragments. To put the
matter another way: Lucy thinks of the defeat of the nun as
the destruction of her love for Paul, just as the earlier burial
of the letters stood for the triumph over her passion for John,
but actually in both cases what is destroyed is only what is
unsound. 'Still mystified, beyond expression, but as
thoroughly, as suddenly, relieved from all sense of the spectral and unearthly', Lucy, who is 'worn out by many nights'
vigils', is able at last to sleep.

But, as the burial of the letters has not totally prevented

[1] Miss Brontë's association of the dormitory at the Pension Héger with what
Miss Ratchford calls the 'dream world' of her imagination is indicated by a
letter to Branwell from Brussels: 'It is a curious metaphysical fact that always in
the evening when I am in the great dormitory alone, having no other company
than a number of beds with white curtains, I always recur as fanatically as ever
to the old ideas, the old faces, and the old scenes in the world below.' [Shorter,
I:267.]

her from feeling subsequent pangs of passion for John, so the destruction of the nun cannot completely preclude the recurrence of Lucy's jealousy of Paul, a jealousy to be conquered only by the full confidence of love. Even in the little house in the Faubourg Clotilde Lucy must forbid Justine Marie her hospitality: 'Warm, jealous, and haughty, I knew not till now that my nature had such a mood; he gathered me near his heart. I was full of faults; he took them and me all home. For the moment of utmost mutiny, he reserved the one deep spell of peace [his declaration of love].' [Chap. 41, III:341.] In this novel Miss Brontë has come to terms with the mixed nature of man, and she is not postulating ideal characters in a flawless world. Lucy's life is to have none of the tinsel of the theatre, no spectral figures, no high romance; nor is there any suggestion that, like Jane Eyre, she has perfected the fusion of emotion and reason. The love of Lucy and Paul is firmly rooted in the imperfections of the world, but it is, for all that, a union that makes the other loves in the novel trivial: 'The love born of beauty was not mine; I had nothing in common with it: I could not dare to meddle with it, but another love, venturing diffidently into life after long acquaintance, furnace-tried by pain, stamped by constancy, consolidated by affection's pure and durable alloy, submitted by intellect to intellect's own tests, and finally wrought up, by his own process, to his own unflawed completeness, this Love that laughed at Passion, his fast frenzies and his hot and hurried extinction, in *this* Love I had a vested interest.' [Chap. 39, III:296.]

The development of the theme of self-knowledge and the knowledge of others does not move forward by a series of scenes as the theme of rationality-*vs.*-emotion does, although the two operate together, as has been suggested.[1] The

[1] Symbolically, the difficulty for Lucy of knowing the nature of those around her is indicated by the multiplicity of names by which the various characters are known. Young Bretton is variously called Graham in his domestic aspect. Isidore as Ginevra's suitor, John in his adult, professional role. Polly Home becomes the Countess Paulina Mary Home de Bassompierre, and ultimately, of course, Mrs. Bretton. M. Paul most often speaks of himself as Emanuel and on occasion has the full, sonorous name of Paul Carl David Emanuel.

development of the two sides of Lucy's psyche naturally contributes to her self-knowledge, and in such scenes as those in the gallery and the theatre, she learns as much of Paul and John as she does of herself. In general, however, her knowledge of others comes slowly, and its growth is only to be seen in comparisons from widely separated sections of the book. As Lucy learns that emotion and rationality must live hand-in-hand, so she must learn that strong initial impressions are often wrong, and that a total reaction from them may be equally invalid, for most persons are mixtures of good and bad. The complexity of human nature is not to be measured by a single phrase, nor is any one person's view of another necessarily just. John, for instance, is no more 'very perfect', as Polly finds him, than he is the foolish weakling that Ginevra takes him for. Lucy finds that he is neither the 'handsome, faithless-looking' lad she first believes him to be nor the prince of men that he later seems, but a very human mixture of the trivial, the snobbish, the generous, and the manly, who improves with age: 'He did not with time degenerate; his faults decayed, his virtues ripened; he rose in intellectual refinement, he won in moral profit: all dregs filtered away, the clear wine settled bright and tranquil.' [Chap. 37, iii:232.]

It is Lucy's own changing and maturing perceptions that are responsible for the apparently contradictory views of John that we see, not inherent change in his character. 'Reader, if, in the course of this work, you find that my opinion of Dr. John undergoes modification, excuse the seeming inconsistency,' she warns us. 'I give the feeling as at the time I felt it; I describe the view of character as it appeared when discovered.' [Chap. 18, ii:55.]

Miss Brontë's letter to George Smith about the third volume discounts the feeling that many readers have had (presumably Smith among them), that Dr. John is the natural hero of the novel and that M. Paul is almost an afterthought: 'Lucy must not marry Dr. John; he is far too youthful, handsome, bright-spirited, and sweet-tempered; he is a "curled darling" of Nature and of Fortune, and must draw a prize in life's lottery. His wife must be young, rich, pretty; he must be made very happy indeed.' [Gaskell, Chap. 25, ii:265.] The clue to her attitude is surely in the phrase 'curled darling', which reduces him to the stature that she imputes to her feminine characters by calling them 'wax dolls'. 'Make your need known, his hand was open,' Lucy observes of him. 'Put your grief into words, he turned no deaf ear. Expect refinements of perception, miracles of intuition, and realize disappointment.' [Chap. 18, ii:51-2.] True maturity of affection for John grows as Lucy learns to recognize that he is far from perfect but that his limitations do not make him less deserving of affection. John does not arrive at an equally clear-sighted assessment of Lucy: 'I realized his entirely misapprehension of my character and nature. He wanted always to give me a rôle not mine. Nature and I opposed him. He did not at all guess what I felt: he did not read my eyes, or face, or gestures; though, I doubt not, all spoke.' [Chap. 27, ii:310.]

Polly, whom Lucy finds so despicable at Bretton, is a self-composed young lady when seen at the theatre; she becomes 'the young Countess . . . a little proud, a little fastidious' [Chap. 26, ii:282] with the German mistress, and when Lucy at La Terrasse is jealous of her, she sees Polly as a kitten, a 'Highland fairy', and a spoiled child 'that longs for some prohibited dainty'. Her essential childishness is shown in her recurrent lisp. The combination of Polly's unformed beauty and her doglike devotion to John is accurately, if ungenerously, indicated by Lucy's description of M. Paul's spaniel, Sylvie, with her master: 'She was very tiny, and had the prettiest little innocent face, the silkiest long ears, the finest dark eyes in the world. I never saw her, but I thought of Paulina de Bassompierre: forgive the association, reader, it *would* occur.' [Chap. 36, iii:190.] Like Caroline Helstone or Rosamond Oliver, Polly is pretty, charming, and a bit

vacuous. As Lucy matures, she becomes increasingly charitable, although not less clear-sighted, in her views of Polly.
Each person, Miss Brontë seems to say, shows many aspects,
and each observer sees what he wishes to see. 'She [Polly]
had different moods for different people. With her father she
really was still a child, or child-like, affectionate, merry and
playful. With me she was serious, and as womanly as thought
and feeling could make her. With Mrs. Bretton she was
docile and reliant, but not expansive. With Graham she was
shy, at present very shy; at moments she tried to be cold; on
occasion she endeavoured to shun him.' [Chap. 26, ii:274.]

Ginevra Fanshawe, the incarnation of impulsive, unintelligent, vain self-will (the mirror opposite of the cold, ruth-
less,   intelligent–and   equally   self-willed–Mme.   Beck),
prompts Lucy early in the book to the observation that there
is in persons of her 'light, careless temperament, and fair,
fragile style of beauty, an entire incapacity to endure: they
seem to sour in adversity, like small-beer in thunder: the
man who takes such a woman for his wife, ought to be prepared to guarantee her an existence all sunshine'. [Chap. 6,
i:105.] It takes Lucy the length of the novel to discover that
her own asperity to Ginevra is perhaps as objectionable as
the younger girl's selfishness, and that at least in the matter
of good temper she is Ginevra's inferior.

Of all her judgments of others, the most important and
most difficult for Lucy is that of M. Paul, for upon that judgment her knowledge of her own identity ultimately rests. Her
growth of understanding of John, Polly, Ginevra, Mme.
Beck, and Père Silas are but parallels to learning to appreciate
Paul. Generous or conceited; masculine or womanish; gentle
or venomous; mild intellectual or black and sallow tiger;
least doctrinaire of men or bigoted child of the Church: what
is the truth of the Professor? Lucy learns to accept that all
these descriptions have a measure of validity. Her first
description of him, although it fails to include the qualities
for which she comes to love him, is still fair to one aspect of

his character: 'A dark little man he certainly was; pungent
and austere. Even to me he seemed a harsh apparition, with
his close-shorn, black head, his broad, sallow brow, his thin
cheek, his wide and quivering nostril, his thorough glance and
hurried bearing. Irritable he was; one heard that, as he
apostrophised with vehemence the awkward squad under his
orders.' [Chap. 14, I:252.] This early view of him is as
accurate–and as partial–as Lucy's assessment of him after
her visit to the Rue des Mages, when she longs to trace in
his countenance 'the imprint of that primitive devotedness,
the signs of that half-knightly, half-saintly chivalry which the
priest's narrative imputed to his nature. He had become my
Christian hero: under that character I wanted to view him.'
[Chap. 35, III:154–5.] The account of his quiet, almost
secret acts of charity has made Lucy come dangerously close
to over-valuing him because of the contrast between his
character and that of Dr. John, for whom it is not enough 'to
satisfy himself . . . society must approve–the world must
admire what he did, or he counted his measures false and
futile.' [Chap. 32,III: 95–6.] The truth of the matter is that
M. Paul is, as Miss Brontë told Smith, 'a man in whom there
is much to forgive, much to "put up with".' [Gaskell, Chap.
25, II:265.]

As Lucy can love Polly and John without losing sight of
their faults, so the mature love of a mate, into which she
grows, knows him by both rationality and emotion, recognizing that he is neither spitting tiger-cat nor white knight:
'Once–unknown, and unloved, I held him harsh and strange;
the low stature, the wiry make, the angles, the darkness, the
manner, displeased me. Now, penetrated with his influence,
and living by his affection, having his worth by intellect, and
his goodness by heart–I preferred him before all humanity.'
[Chap. 41, III:343.]

It is, however, the problem of Lucy's own identity that is
paramount in the novel, and both the other characters and
Lucy herself err in seeing the truth of that identity. 'Who *are*

you, Miss Snowe?' asks Ginevra in perplexity at finding the
English dragon, known to her as Timon, Diogenes, or
Crusty, may have a personality and a background of unsus-
pected depth. 'But *are* you anybody?' she persists, putting
into literal, direct words the problem that occupies Lucy so
long. For Ginevra, as for Mme. Beck and Dr. John, the
question is, however, really one of mere social standing.
Mme. Beck 'had never from the first treated me otherwise
than with respect; and when she found that I was liable to
frequent invitations from a chateau and a great hotel,
respect improved into distinction'. [Chap. 26, II: 259.]
John's manner to her, Lucy believes, would have been quite
different had she 'been intrinsically the same, but possessing
the additional advantages of wealth and station. . . .'
[Chap. 27, II:305.]

To all but one pair of eyes the essential Lucy is figuratively
as invisible and unrecognizable as she is literally on the
night of the carnival when she passes unnoticed before the
eyes of her acquaintances: 'Madame Beck esteemed me
learned and blue; Miss Fanshawe, caustic, ironic, and cynical;
Mr. Home, a model teacher, the essence of the sedate and
discreet: somewhat conventional perhaps, too strict, limited
and scrupulous, but still the pink and pattern of governess-
correctness; whilst another person, Professor Paul Emanuel
to wit, never lost an opportunity of intimating his opinion
that mine was rather a fiery and rash nature—adventurous,
indocile, and audacious.' [Chap. 26, II:278.] M. Paul,
although quick at misunderstanding Lucy's motives, is the
one person who sees her clearly, from the time he tries his
'skill at physiognomy' on her: 'he meant to see through me,
and . . . a veil would be no veil for him.' [Chap. 7, I:125.]
Olympian, he sits in his window overlooking the school
garden: 'My book is this garden; its contents are human
nature—female human nature. I know you all by heart.'
[Chap. 31, III:83.]

Of Lucy's background we are told almost nothing,

although we infer that she is an orphan, since she makes her childhood home with kinsfolk. In the search for her own identity, Lucy attempts to become one of the family at La Terrasse, with her god-mother taking the place of a mother and John becoming a brother—and more—to her. The superficial reasons for her attempt at identification with the Brettons are obvious, for they have the familiarity of long acquaintance, a community of background and nationality. But her endeavour to become a Bretton is as immature *au fond* as Lucy's passion for John, and as if to indicate the fact, Miss Brontë constantly emphasizes that her convalescence at La Terrasse, with all its mementoes of the English house at Bretton is a metaphorical return to childhood. The surroundings are the same, Mrs. Bretton unchanged in appearance and treatment of her son, John changed only by the addition of a beard, and Lucy remains what she has been as a girl, a welcome guest but not of the family.

Everything at La Terrasse that seems conducive to its becoming home to Lucy is summed up in the punning significance of the name Bretton. In this novel, where things are seldom what they seem, the name becomes ironic, for Lucy is to find identity, family, and home where all at first seems alien: 'I was conscious of rapport between you and myself,' Paul tells her. 'You are patient, and I am choleric; you are quiet and pale, and I am tanned and fiery; you are a strict Protestant, and I am a sort of lay Jesuit: but we are alike— there is affinity. Do you see it, mademoiselle, when you look in the glass? Do you observe that your forehead is shaped like mine--that your eyes are cut like mine? Do you hear that you have some of my tones of voice? Do you know that you have many of my looks? I perceive all this, and believe that you were born under my star. Yes, you were born under my star! Tremble! for where that is the case with mortals, the threads of their destinies are difficult to disentangle; knottings and catchings occur—sudden breaks leave damage in the web.' [Chap. 31, III:90–91.]

'Petite sœur' Paul calls Lucy at the breakfast in the country, and later he asks her: 'Will Miss Lucy be the sister of a very poor, fettered, burdened, encumbered man?' [Chap. 35, III:171.] In his subsequent gentleness to her Lucy finds occasion to wonder: 'Could it be that he was becoming more than friend or brother?' [Chap. 38, III:242.]

As Lucy has learned painfully that the Brettons are not her family, so she learns at last that Paul's true family is not his cousin, Mme. Beck, his god-child Justine, his former tutor, the woman for whom he takes the place of son-in-law, or even his Mother Church. The consanguinity of love is greater than that of family.

The house in the Faubourg Clotilde becomes at last the emblem of the identity towards which Lucy has been groping throughout her life, for it is her true home, and in it she has found definition. Neither English nor totally Labassecourien, the little house has finally resolved the polarity of La Terrasse and the dark house of the Rue des Mages, the worlds of the unfeeling reason and the irrational imagination, the Puritan severity of Protestantism and the warm piety of Roman Catholicism. Externals no longer count; reality has taken the place of appearance. The meaning of 'identity' has become a kind of pun: individual identity can be found only in identity with another. 'He deemed me born under his star: he seemed to have spread over me its beam like a banner.' [Chap. 41, III:343.] To Lucy's plea for reassurance that she is physically attractive to Paul, he gives 'a short, strong answer –an answer which silenced, subdued, yet profoundly satisfied. Ever after that, I knew what I was for *him*; and what I might be for the rest of the world, I ceased painfully to care.' [Chap. 41, III:326.]

In the hushed isolation of the little house all barriers between Lucy and Paul finally fall: differences in religion, language, nationality, age, and background all become mere externals with no final meaning. The ultimate unity between the lovers is foreshadowed throughout the book by their slow and painful attempts to learn toleration of each other's religion. Lucy knows to the end that 'God is not with Rome', and Paul can never totally understand Lucy's 'strange, self-reliant, invulnerable creed', but she learns that '*this* Romanist held the purer elements of his creed with an innocency of heart which God must love', [Chap. 36, III: 197] and Paul is 'made thoroughly to feel that Protestants were not necessarily the irreverent Pagans his director had insinuated'. [Chap. 36, III: 195.] As Lucy has not been able to believe in great differences between the Protestant denominations, so Paul finally expresses the pettiness of differences even between Protestant and Roman Catholic: 'How seem in the eyes of that God who made all firmaments, from whose nostrils issued whatever of life is here, or in the stars shining yonder – how seem the differences of man?' [Chap. 36, III: 203.]

' "Remain a Protestant," ' Paul tells Lucy before leaving Villette. ' "My little English Puritan, I love Protestantism in you. I own its severe charm. There is something in its ritual I cannot receive myself, but it is the sole creed for "Lucy".'

'All Rome could not put into him bigotry, nor the Propaganda itself make him a real Jesuit. He was born honest, and not false – artless, and not cunning – a freeman, and not a slave. His tenderness had rendered him ductile in a priest's hands, his affection, his devotedness, his sincere pious enthusiasm blinded his kind eyes sometimes, made him abandon justice to himself to do the work of craft, and serve the ends of selfishness; but these are faults so rare to find, so costly to their owner to indulge, we scarcely know whether they will not one day be reckoned amongst the jewels.' [Chap. 42, III: 347–8.] The simple meal served on the balcony of Lucy's new home becomes almost a sacramental experience of a shared religious sense that lies beyond sect.[1]

---

[1] Although this is the most conspicuous example in the book of a fairly common usage of shared meals as indication of personal harmony, throughout Miss Brontë displays a somewhat unusual interest in the reconciliatory, even amatory, powers of food. The child Polly shows her love for her father and Graham by wheedling special goodies for them; Lucy expresses her preference for

With her final clear-eyed recognition of her own nature and that of Paul, with the question of her identity solved, Lucy has changed from the cold, self-regarding Miss Snowe to the fulfilled spiritual mate of her tutor, assured of her place in the universe. The ambiguous ending, with its unwillingness to trouble sunny imaginations by speaking directly of Paul's death, is Miss Brontë's last refusal to bow to the dictates of romantic fiction.[1] The spirit of love is more important than 'union and a happy succeeding life'. Reality, as Lucy has finally learned, is what matters, not appearance.

Ginevra by sharing part of her own portion of breakfast with her and by drinking from the same cup. Lucy and Paul are several times reconciled by gifts of food; Lucy's rebelliousness as she is preparing for the play is stilled by the cakes and coffee that Paul brings her; on the occasion of the May outing their quarrel is healed by the breakfast that Paul provides; his offer of friendship is often expressed by chocolate comfits and shared brioches.

[1] Mrs. Gaskell tells us that Miss Brontë's father specifically asked that the novel have a happy ending, but 'the idea of M. Paul Emanuel's death at sea was stamped on her imagination till it assumed the distinct force of reality; and she could no more alter her fictitious ending than if they had been facts which she was relating. All she could do in compliance with her father's wish was so to veil the fate in oracular words, as to leave it to the character and discernment of her readers to interpret her meaning.' [Gaskell, Chap. 25, ii:266.] In a heavily facetious letter to George Smith, Miss Brontë indicated that drowning would be a happier fate for Paul than marriage to 'that–person–that–that–individual–"Lucy Snowe".–' [SHB, iv:56.]

CRITICAL BIBLIOGRAPHY

The following are but a few of the many criticisms of Miss Brontë's works. They are chosen because they seem especially illuminating or provocative about her technique as novelist.

Bentley, Phyllis: *The Brontës* (Home and Van Thal, London, 1947).

Cecil, David: *Early Victorian Novelists: Essays in Revaluation* (Constable and Co., London, 1934).

Chase, Richard: 'The Brontës, or Myth Domesticated,' in *Forms of Modern Fiction*, ed. William Van O'Connor (University of Minnesota Press, Minneapolis, 1948).

Colby, Robert A.: *'Villette* and the Life of the Mind,' *PMLA*, September 1960, pp. 410–19.

Davis, Joe Lee: introduction to *Jane Eyre* (Rinehart and Co., New York, 1950).

Day, Martin S.: 'Central Concepts of *Jane Eyre*,' *Personalist*, October 1960, pp. 495–505.

Dunbar, Georgia S.: 'Proper Names in *Villette*,' *Nineteenth-Century Fiction*, June 1960, pp. 77–80.

Heilman, Robert B.: 'Charlotte Brontë's "New Gothic",' in *From Jane Austen to Joseph Conrad*, ed. Robert C. Rathburn and Martin Steinmann, Jr. (University of Minnesota Press, Minneapolis, 1958).

Heilman, Robert B.: 'Charlotte Brontë, Reason, and the Moon,' *Nineteenth-Century Fiction*, March 1960, pp. 283–302.

Korg, Jacob: 'The Problem of Unity in *Shirley*,' *Nineteenth-Century Fiction*, September 1957, pp. 125–136.

Prescott, Joseph: '*Jane Eyre:* A Romantic Exemplum with a Difference,' in *Twelve Original Essays on Great English Novels*, ed. Charles Shapiro (Wayne State University Press, Detroit, 1960).

Ratchford, Fannie Elizabeth: *The Brontës' Web of Childhood* (Columbia University Press, New York, 1941).

Scargill, M. H.: ' "All Passion Spent": A Revaluation of *Jane Eyre*,' *University of Toronto Quarterly*, January 1950, pp. 120–25.

Senseman, Wilfred M.: 'Charlotte Brontë's Use of Physiognomy and Phrenology,' *Papers of the Michigan Academy of Science, Arts, and Letters*, pp. 475–86.

Tillotson, Kathleen: '*Jane Eyre*,' in *Novels of the Eighteen-Forties* (Clarendon Press, Oxford, 1954).

BRITISH LITERATURE
IN NORTON PAPERBOUND EDITIONS

Jane Austen   *Emma*   (A Norton Critical Edition, edited by Stephen Parrish)
   Persuasion
   Pride and Prejudice   (A Norton Critical Edition, edited by
      Donald Gray)

Robert Browning   *The Ring and the Book*

Emily Brontë   *Wuthering Heights*   (A Norton Critical Edition, edited by
      William M. Sale, Jr.)

Anthony Burgess   *A Clockwork Orange*
   Tremor of Intent

Fanny Burney   *Evelina*

Joseph Conrad   *Heart of Darkness*   (A Norton Critical Edition, edited by
      Robert Kimbrough)
   Lord Jim   (A Norton Critical Edition, edited by Thomas Moser)

Charles Dickens   *Great Expectations*   (A Norton Critical Edition, edited by
      Edgar Rosenberg)
   Hard Times   (A Norton Critical Edition, edited by
      George Ford and Sylvère Monod)

John Donne   *John Donne's Poetry*   (A Norton Critical Edition, selected and
      edited by A. L. Clements)

Maria Edgeworth   *Castle Rackrent*

Henry Fielding   *Joseph Andrews*

Mrs. Gaskell   *Mary Barton*

Edmund Gosse   *Father and Son*

Thomas Hardy   *Tess of the D'Urbervilles*   (A Norton Critical Edition, edited by
      Scott Elledge)

Henry Mackenzie   *The Man of Feeling*

Thomas Love Peacock   *Nightmare Abbey*

Samuel Richardson   *Pamela*

William Shakespeare   *Hamlet*   (A Norton Critical Edition, edited by Cyrus Hoy)
   Henry IV, Part I   (A Norton Critical Edition, edited by
      James L. Sanderson)

Jonathan Swift   *Gulliver's Travels*   (A Norton Critical Edition, edited by
      Robert A. Greenberg)

Anthony Trollope   *The Last Chronicle of Barset*

NORTON CRITICAL EDITIONS